time. While the local commu
home and holiday industry the
when they too adjust to the c
noises and different pace and c

It is best not to be in too much of a hurry in Norfolk and, if tempted to queue barge, be aware that the informally dressed 'local' in the queue in front may well be a High Court judge or Fellow of the Royal Society. Appearances are deceptive in the countryside. As one resident put it, 'Some visitors seem to think we are yokels with hay sticking out of one ear and straw out of the other.' North Norfolk has a rich mixture of characters, whether they have lived here all their lives, or moved in with their wealth and talent because they have come to appreciate this very special part of England.

As for the memories themselves, these can fade as the years advance and take on an element of myth, or be vested with enchantment and embellishment. Whilst striving for accuracy, I hope my readers will accept that the human memory is fallible. It is all the more interesting for that. Writers who try to achieve infallibility either never start, or are less likely to finish, writing a book. They suffer from the same condition as the darts player who cannot let go of the dart. There is a sense of urgency about recording the memories of people of advancing age. I want them to have some years to enjoy seeing themselves in print while readers find pleasure in sharing those experiences.

Telling the tale is one thing but seeing one's own words in print for the first time is another. I am grateful to the contributors to this book for their help as we worked together on the finished chapters.

Raymond Monbiot

Eastgate House
Burnham Market

By the same author

The Burnham Book of Characters and Memories

Characters of North Norfolk

Website: www.raymondmonbiotbooks.co.uk

Raymond Monbiot

MORE Characters of North Norfolk

Compiled by Raymond Monbiot

Published in 2006 by:

Rotherfield Management Ltd
Eastgate House
Burnham Market
Norfolk
PE31 8HH

ISBN 0 9542567 2 7

ISBN 978 0 9542567 2 2

Typesetting:
Raymond Monbiot

Printed by:
Barnwell's Print Ltd.,
Penfold Street,
Aylsham, Norfolk
NR11 6ET
Tel: 01263 732767

CONTENTS

Page

Foreword

In 1966 a woman aged 106 recalled the account of the Battle of Waterloo, as told her by her grandfather, who fought in the Duke of Wellington's army in 1815. On the morning after the battle the field was white - the last sight one would have imagined - but it was the result of the cotton wads of the cartridges lying thick upon the ground.

This kindled my interest in living history. This is my third book in this series following the success of the first two: *The Burnhams Book of Characters and Memories* and *Characters of North Norfolk*. Most of the men and women whose stories I have published have lived in North Norfolk for most, if not all, of their lives. Their memories stretch back in some cases over 70 years. However, these have rarely, if ever, been committed to paper and there was a danger that they would be lost forever.

This book is about real people who have lived and worked in North Norfolk through good times and bad. Peter Scoles has worked all his career with young people, many underprivileged, and at one point wrote a passion play which was staged in St George's Chapel, Windsor. Mike Cringle farmed in Kenya at the time of the Mau Mau and returned to his native North Norfolk to marry Anne, who was a founder of the Burnham Market Craft Fair. Together they set up an antiques business and have been at the heart of village activity for 40 years. Nigel Benbow was a bait digger at Stiffkey before becoming the greengrocer in Fakenham and Holt. Brian Farrow is a founder member of the Sheringham Shantymen. Larry Randall is Mr Fixit of Cromer. These are just five examples of the 11 compelling chapters in **MORE** *Characters of North Norfolk*.

There was severe hardship in North Norfolk in the 1920s and 30s when the struggle to raise a family and make ends meet, with no state help, meant the larger the family the poorer they tended to be. Feeding and clothing six, eight or more children, on an agricultural wage, forged inter-dependence, strength of character, a sense of community and fear of eviction through being unable to pay the weekly rent of two shillings and sixpence. But Norfolk men and women are tenacious and staunch. Field Marshal Montgomery maintained that to take a position he would look to the Scots or the Welsh, but to hold a position he would look to the East Anglians.

North Norfolk has changed a good deal over the last 60 years. Reliance on horses gave way to machinery just before the Second World War. In the post-war years the amount of labour required on the farms was drastically reduced. Where a farm in the 1930s could field one or more cricket teams, this all changed with the advent of machinery. Cottages lay empty and decaying and there were no longer throngs of children in the streets. When the railway closed to passenger traffic, following the North Sea floods of 1953, and freight traffic ceased a decade later, the lifeline to the outside world was cut.

The motor car was not yet in general use and a long chapter in the lives of the true villagers closed. From the age of 11 many of them had travelled to school by train to Wells and Fakenham from the surrounding district, and goods were moved to and from communities by train. Many villages and much of the property fell into a sorry state.

Then in the 1970s Norfolk was discovered as a jewel for holidays and second homes. Property was bought up by Londoners and other 'furriners' and 'blow ins' at prices well beyond the means of local people. But new industries flourished. Builders, plumbers and decorators became ever more in demand. A new generation of shops opened to satisfy the needs of busy second-homers who used their leisure time to buy sophisticated clothes and home furnishings locally. Shopping at the weekend, when there is more time available than in the working week, has encouraged some fashionable boutiques to flourish, notably in Blakeney, Holt and Burnham Market. An abundance of good eating places followed and North Norfolk is as well served for eating out as any rural area in the country.

Whilst the true villagers may regret the passing of the old days, few want to return to fetching water in a bucket from the pump, to emptying it and the contents of the outside loo into a hole in the garden, or to a nightly visit from the 'honey cart', or to the hard grind of manual labour that was the daily norm. However, adjustment to new realities is not made easier by the enormous increase in traffic and pressure on amenities, especially in the summer. In Burnham Market 68 per cent of houses are second homes and empty most of the

About the Author

Raymond Monbiot was born in 1937, went to school in London and started work as a trainee with J. Lyons & Co. in 1956 humping sacks of flour for the bakery. Trained as a pastry chef, where his duties included making the cakes for Buckingham Palace garden parties, he moved into production management which included being a foreman on the nightshift, became a van salesman and rose in the ranks to be the national sales manager of Lyons Bakery at the age of 24. He managed companies for Lyons until he became managing director of Huntley & Palmers, Jacobs and Peek Frean biscuits and later chief executive of Campbells Soups at King's Lynn. He is a liveryman of the Worshipful Company of Butchers, a freeman of the City of London and, for his political and public services, was awarded the MBE in 1981 and the CBE in 1994. He was for many years a columnist and contributor to trade magazines. His first book – *How to Manage Your Boss* – sold 30,000 copies, and his first two books about North Norfolk – *The Burnhams Book of Characters and Memories* and *Characters of North Norfolk* - have been very successful.

In 1961 he married Rosalie Gresham Cooke whose father was a Member of Parliament and whose family has owned the Friary at Blakeney since 1911 – managed today by her brother, the Revd Hereward Cooke, canon of Norwich cathedral and a Norwich city councillor. Rosalie is Norfolk county councillor for the Docking division and cabinet member for children's services. She is a board member of

Peddars Way Housing Association. She was awarded the OBE in 1992.

They live in Burnham Market and have two surviving children. George Monbiot is a well known environmental activist, journalist, columnist and author. Eleanor, who lives in Kenya, is world wide director of humanitarian learning for World Vision, the second largest humanitarian aid organisation in the world. She was awarded the OBE at the age of 34 in 2005. Katherine died at the age of 31 in 1997.

Rosalie Monbiot OBE

Burnham Market

Peter Scoles

Peter Scoles was born at number 8 Church Walk, Burnham Market in 1935. He is one of a family of five – four boys: Ray, Billy and Phillip, and their sister Pauline. Father, Joseph, was miller at Roy's Mill, and their mother, Violet, after working initially in 'service', worked hard all her life to supplement the income and support the large family.

"An early recollection was an outbreak of diphtheria when I was four or five at the beginning of the war and some of the family had to go to the isolation hospital in Dereham. I nearly died as I was unable to breathe. Dad, who had fought in the First World War, cycled over to visit us, but was not allowed in and had to see us through the windows. As he cycled home he was shot at by a German plane. Many years later I revisited the hospital, now an office, and recalled the smell of chloroform. This was administered by a mask over the face with no pre-med injection. The slab on which I had my operation was still on view.

"On Sundays my parents 'encouraged' me to walk with them to Norton churchyard where members of our family were buried, or to look at the graves of the fresh buried. Then we would walk to Granny and Granddad Jack Bean's at 19 Creake Road for our tea where we ate winkles and cockles and a cold rice pudding, set really hard in a white enamel basin. The winkles were retrieved from their shells with either a dressmaking or hat pin.

"At the age of five I went to Burnham infants school and enjoyed happy times under Miss Whitton. We were given slates to write on with sticks of white chalk. If we pressed too hard the chalk would break. 'Religion' was among the subjects taught and I joined the trebles in the choir at St Mary's church, Burnham Westgate. From an early age the church was a part of my life. When I moved on to join the 'big boys' in the middle school, it was realised that I had musical ability. It was suggested that I go to Norwich Cathedral School but this would have meant staying away from home and as usual my parents could not afford it. At 11 years old I didn't pass the scholarship to Fakenham grammar school.

Peter and sister Pauline

"As children we got up to pranks such as putting penny coins on the railway line so the train could flatten them. More serious, in Mother's judgement, was when we stretched cotton across the railway line to stop the train. The crime was that we were wasting her valuable darning cotton and as punishment she stopped my comics – the *Beano* and *Radio Fun*. One night PC Snelling called at the front door and asked me directly if I had put paraffin in the Norton church font. I had done no such thing – but why should he think I had?

"I enjoyed written English, then known then as 'composition', and when I left school at 15 I wanted to be a journalist. There was an opening at the *Norfolk Chronicle* but again this would have meant staying away from home. I had to get a job locally and my first one was as an errand boy at International Stores in Burnham Market. Saturday was the worst. My 'Granville' bike was loaded so high that I could hardly see over the handle bars. Some of the customers' orders got a bit crushed and they would moan at me if the biscuits were broken. The Burnham Overy delivery was most tasking – in all weathers biking up New Road, up 'the Gong' and back to the International in time for 5.30 p.m. closing.

"I was approached to take an apprenticeship. I had no idea what this meant but Mother said it would do me good to learn to be a grocer. The area manager for International Stores was Mr Hindley and I knew he was important when he called at our house because Mother received him in the front room. This was usually reserved for weddings and funerals so Mr Hindley had to be something special. I was given a paper to sign and was thus indentured as a grocer on a two-year apprenticeship at International Stores.

"The staff in the store in those days wore long white aprons. Nothing was pre-packed, bacon was sliced on a

Berkel machine, sugar and butter were weighed out from bulk. Dates were the worst because they were sticky. One of my jobs was to keep the rats under control. This was done with cardboard smeared with 'rat sticker' to which the rat stuck until I hit it on the head to kill it. I would then burn the cardboard and the rat on the fire. One had to be alert, the rats got everywhere. Jill Walker, grocery assistant from Stanhoe, got the shock of her life when she reached up to get spice from a high shelf and a rat jumped over her shoulder.

"Our next-door neighbour, Mr Hazel, the coalman, would moan that he had to sit next to a hole in the wall and kill mice from 'your shop'. We had a cat but it was useless. Part of the training I did not like was when Mr Hindley (I did not like him either because he called me Sonny) pretended to be a customer and I had to prepare his order, weighing out a quarter pound of tea, half a pound of sugar, biscuits from a tin and, worst of all, an ounce of pepper. I had to make a cone of paper but the loose pepper always trickled out of the bottom. I failed that test.

"Mr Hindley would ask me what was on promotion under the 'Mitre' brand name because I was supposed to sell this to the customers, whether they wanted it or not. Then I had to price and total up the bill and make out a voucher for that amount, which the customer was supposed to hand to the cashier and pay on the way out. When a customer left the shop without paying there was an enquiry of the staff to find out who made up that order and help to identify the customer. This all added to the complication of post-war shortages. There was a lot of trade 'under the counter' after the war, where favoured customers could obtain cigarettes – discreetly. 'Have you got any Players or Woodbines?' ' I'll have to find out, Sir……..' The cashier inspector was Miss Sexton. Until I was 17 I earned 15 shillings a week and had to give Mother some of that. I had to canvas new customers by knocking on doors which I hated doing because I was no good at it.

"Mother was keen that I should learn to play a musical instrument. I chose the violin, not least because the teacher, Miss Carter, owned a sweet shop in the Market Place, through which we had to pass to her parlour where lessons were held. Sweets were still on ration at the time and a picking on the way out was appreciated. I didn't have a music stand and used the crockery dresser instead. The cups would be removed from their hooks and the music score hung on them. Despite regular family complaints about my squeaking noises as I learned the violin, I none the less was eventually considered good enough to join the Labour concert party, known as the 'Evereadys', which rehearsed in the Old Black Horse pub – now a gift and antiques shop. All our concerts started with 'Here we are again' and finished with 'Now is the Hour'.

"The 'Eveready' pianist was Mrs Terrington from Burnham Thorpe and we travelled all over North Norfolk in a bus, giving concerts in village halls, for example at Binham and Warham. I joined the Burnham Market choral society under the direction of Nancy Peacock, a very fierce lady from Sunderland Farm, which was off a track up the Whiteway

Road. We had a wide repertoire. We performed Edward German's *Merrie England* and oratorios such as Handel's *Messiah* for which we joined with other choral societies. We performed in Norwich and also in the Marble Hall at Holkham. I did not play my violin on these occasions! My repertoire was restricted to Stanchen's 'Serenade' and Schubert's 'Serenade'.

"There were other International Stores staff in the church choir: Eileen Bouch, who became a Ringwood when she married, and Evelyn Scribbans and Bertie Elvin, a robust tenor. It was hard work – we sang three times a day on a Sunday. I and my brothers took turns at pumping the organ which relied on this ancient method for its wind. There was a wind indicator, a dangling plumb line, showing when we should pump, and, in devilment, we would bait the organist, Joyce Curzon – later Farrow – by letting the wind go right down. She would get agitated, putting her head through the curtain, and tell us to pump properly and we would do so jerkily so the organ made a fitful noise. Then she would hiss, 'I'll tell your mother.' As far as I know she never did.

"Mother was the rock – she was our mother ship and she worked hard, continually taking jobs like washing, making gloves from rabbit skins, salting hams and keeping house. We had an outdoor wash house where on Saturday bath day a corn sack was put across the window for modesty. We shared the bath water which had to be drawn from outside water butts and heated in the copper over the fire. The lucky one was the first in the bath. We had a coal house and a separate privy. This was opposite the lavatory of the house next door and we would sit there having conversations, with the door open, with our neighbour, Charlie Curzon, the cobbler at number 9.

It was the time of newspaper rather than toilet paper, except when Mother's posh relatives came up from London, because she believed they were used to something better, such as a flush toilet, coming as they did from Stoke Newington, N16. Prior to their visit she would distemper the lavatory and scrub the seat. She dreaded the visit of the night cart man, Charlie Laurence, coming in the afternoon, which he occasionally did, rather than at night as was usual. He was prone to spill something and it made a mess, a smell and Mother angry.

"When I visited Roy's Mill where Dad worked, we had to beware of the complex of pulleys and the water wheel. It was a death trap by today's standards. We were not allowed to fish in the trout stream, but there was the staff's wooden privy behind the water wheel from which it was possible to lower a baited line and catch a trout whilst sitting on the seat. Many a time I returned from the mill with a live trout down my shirt. Father would tell me not to do that but he always helped us eat the trout.

"We shared everything in those days – if we caught a rabbit or if we bought herring from the fishermen who came to the village with their carts. We had no inhibitions about gathering fresh dead edible things. We found maggots under dead birds and animals and these were good bait for fishing in Holkham lake. Cowpats were interesting. We would upturn them with sticks to see what creepy crawlies lived underneath.

"My parents would decide on impulse that we would have a chicken for Sunday dinner. That meant catching it, wringing its neck, plucking and cleaning it before getting round to cooking it. Or Father would say he fancied celery in winter and one of us would go with a torch and lift it from the earth. We picked sprouts with the frost on them and they tasted fresher than one could imagine these days when bought vegetables may have travelled halfway round the world. We listened for the chickens to start their clucking after they had laid and we would go and gather the eggs when they were still wet from the laying.

"We caught rabbits with ferrets, which would be starved for a few days before we sent them down the burrows. When harvest was under way we waited until the rabbits had been flushed out from the remaining corn and we would club them. We could keep what we killed but it was important not to upset the farmer by trampling his corn in premature excitement. Then we would 'hull' (gut) them and carry them home hung on a stick. Mr Sherar was one of the farmers whose rabbits we killed at harvest. He was a strong disciplinarian but he and Mrs Sherar were very kind, and when we put on *Aladdin* at All Saints' Hall at St Ethelbert's, they lent me a costume he had brought back from Malaya, to wear for my part as the prince's daughter.

"This was in 1947 when everything was in short supply following the war. The scenery was put together by J. Pike, using coloured cellophane for the windows. Clifford Hewitt played Aladdin's maid, Brian Baldwin was the villain, and Alan and Brian Utting and Trevor Manning were included in the chorus. I became really interested in the performing arts and would do everything I could to earn enough money to go regularly to the Cosy Cinema in Herrings Lane. There were two performances a night, at 5.15 p.m. and at 8.00 p.m. Seats in the front three rows were fivepence and in the balcony two shillings and ninepence. There were prices in between at tenpence, one and threepence, one and ninepence, and two and threepence. We usually sat in the tenpenny seats and as a special treat in the one and ninepennies. The Rose and Crown on the corner of Herrings Lane sold Smiths crisps to eat during the film. They came with salt in a twist of blue paper.

"The pump on the village green, opposite the Rose and Crown, was a major meeting place for the district. Hubbard's bus would pick up cinema goers from the villages around. If we had enough money only to buy a ticket, but not for crisps or a portion of Eldorado ice cream wrapped in wax paper, we would fill our pockets with 'uplifted' apple windfalls from Roy's orchards nearby. The Cosy showed some blockbuster films including *The Charge of the Light Brigade*, *Victoria the Great* and *The Mudlark*. There was usually a 'B' film in addition to the main feature and always a newsreel by which we kept up to date with the progress of the war. The National Anthem was played at the end of the evening performance and we were not allowed out before its last notes were heard.

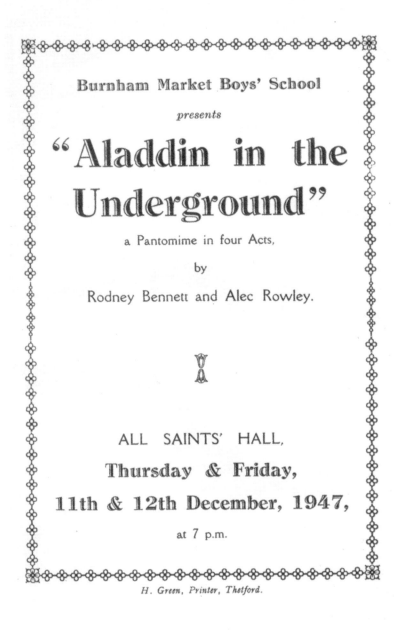

Burnham Market Boys' School

presents

"Aladdin in the Underground"

a Pantomime in four Acts,

by

Rodney Bennett and Alec Rowley.

ALL SAINTS' HALL,

Thursday & Friday,

11th & 12th December, 1947,

at 7 p.m.

H. Green, Printer, Thetford.

Print of Programme

PROGRAMME.

Characters.

WIDOW TWANKEY	... ...	J. Foster
ALADDIN, her son ...	... ...	{ D. Cremer
		{ R. Lack
HOO-ZOO, errand boy	... ...	M. Cremer
ALMANAZOR, the villain	... ...	R. Cardew
A HAWKER, his ally	... ...	B. Baldwin
EMPEROR OF CHINA	... ...	B. Smith
PRINCESS, his daughter	... ...	P. Scoles
AZRA, her maid	... ...	{ L. Sillis
		{ C. Hewitt
CHANCELLOR	... ...	A. Hall
SLAVE OF THE RING	... ...	B. Carter
SLAVE OF THE LAMP	... ...	B. Howell
CHIEF OF THE SPIRITS	... ...	M. Ireson
CHORUS OF WORKERS	{ D. Andrews A. Fenn	D. May
	{ K. Andrews B. Foster	G. Parr
AND	{ B. Baldwin D. Howell	D. Read
ATTENDANTS	{ N. Doy J. Loft	R. Smith
	{ B. Everitt A. Murray	
	{ G. Bond R. Parsons	
CHORUS OF SPIRITS	{ T. Kendal A. Utting	
	{ T. Manning B. Utting	
	{ B. May	

Scenes.

ACT ONE:

The Widow Twankey's Laundry in Pekin.

ACT TWO:

Scene 1. The Well.

Scene 2. The Magic Cave.

ACT THREE:

As Act One.

ACT FOUR:

The Royal Palace.

SCENERY ... by the boys under the direction of Mr. J. Pike.

LIGHTING EFFECTS ... ... by Mr. W. Ives.

STAGING AND PRODUCTION ... ... by the Staff.

We are deeply indebted, in these difficult times, to the friends who have loaned us Costumes and other properties, without which we could not have staged the production.

23

"To earn entrance money to the Cosy, Ronnie Lack, who lived in Station Road, and I, did a number of sessions practising bandaging skills with the Red Cross for sixpence a time. This would pay for a fivepenny seat and a penny bag of broken crisps. We also did chores at home such as shopping, digging the garden, gleaning ears of corn for the chickens, getting the washing in and going up to Grannie Bean's in Creake Road to chop her kindling sticks for the week.

"When I finished my apprenticeship with International Stores I needed a job but I was determined it would not be in the grocery trade. The US Air Force at Sculthorpe were advertising for cleaners to work on the base. The money was good. Because of my grocery retail skills I moved to the PX base supermarket, firstly in the grocery department and eventually in the camera department. No tax was paid on cameras and the range available was such as one could only dream about in post-war Britain. I was able to buy a Bell & Howell camera and this encouraged my entertainment and communication skills. At Christmas the PX, which was huge, put on a store display and I was dressed up as a promotional snowman who had just arrived astride a rocket.

"On one occasion, Jayne Mansfield, the film star, came to start an American football match and I had to take a base newspaper photo which, because of her well endowed shape, caused some difficulty in identifying the ball. There was 'access' to perfume and cigarettes – little wonder the local girls took such an interest in American servicemen. Entertainment was available in Wells where, for example, the Sweet Jivers band performed at dances and American servicemen wooed the local girls, a number of whom became GI brides.

"I organised local community events since leaving school, some of which were quite spectacular, but by no means were they always free of disasters. For example, a waterfall, cleverly constructed on the stage as an essential part of the scenery, collapsed, flooding everything. We had a dance in All Saints Hall – 'up the hut' - where I needed 'Slipparene' for the floor but could not get it and used Oxydol soap powder instead. The combination of this and an over-heated tortoise stove in the corner caused everyone's eyes to water. I poured water on to the stove to cool it down. The combination of this and soap powder produced an eye-watering event.

"At the Burnhams 1953 coronation pageant, when it poured with rain, Roy Stimpson and I acquired some little bottles from the chemist, filled them with innocuous liquid, dressed as monks and sold them as love potions. Roy and I formed a skiffle group in the style of Lonnie Donegan who was all the rage at the time. I played the tea chest, Roy the wash board, and Peter Drake, son of the Hoste Arms landlord, the guitar. We rehearsed in the Hoste barns but did not achieve much acclaim. I was always interested in getting my friends and colleagues to participate in entertainment, particularly for good causes, and I found that organising events was becoming a feature of my life.

"This was recognised, not least by two governors of Burnham Market school, Captain and Mrs Lance, who encouraged me to participate in local events. I was encouraged to apply in 1960 for the youth work two-year course at Westhill Training College at Selly Oak in Birmingham. The only way I could take this up was to apply for a Norfolk county grant, which was successful. I had never been on a course before, nor to Birmingham for that matter, but I had to get there to attend an interview. They talked to me about what I had done in the field of youth work and looked at my references. I passed the interview and got the grant, so in 1960, at the age of 25, I was off to college for two years. Packing up my trunk and getting to Birmingham, all across country, was quite a challenge.

"I met Pat at Westhill. She was on a three-year teaching course and was later to become my wife. She helped me make the grant last and our first date was at a Youth for Christ meeting in Birmingham town hall. My youth course was in 'rough' parts of Birmingham. We were sent climbing in the Peak District, and I had an opportunity to create a coffee bar mural. I did this with springs from a mattress attached to a wall. Assessors of my efforts at the youth club included Sir John Hunt of Mount Everest fame. I passed my final exams with a 'C', which meant pass, and a 'D' which, when I saw it, made my heart fall, but I discovered it signified 'Distinction' in the 'Principle and Practice of Youth Work'.

"After the course was completed I moved to a youth worker job in a combined, ecumenical churches venture in Forest Gate in the East End of London. This was brought together by Baptists, Methodists and Church of England. It called for evangelist ministering to skinheads, mods and rockers with the objective of getting them into church. In the course of my ministering I was hit on the head with a billiard cue. For three years I worked in one of the toughest and most deprived areas of London. I was baptised (for the second time!) in a big pool by total immersion. Some of the onlookers threw pennies and the priest beat me to retrieving them by a short head.

"Pat and I married in 1963. I was 28 and she was 27 and a teacher. Her father had died and her mother decided to go and live in Oregon where Pat's sister, a GI bride, was already established. Pat and I decided we would go and live in Oregon – for a while at least. Pat got a job as a teacher in a Boise elementary school, a tough area where the pupils were predominantly black. I was employed at Meir & Franks departmental store in Portland. I got involved in birthday breakfasts for the staff where bacon and maple syrup were served, and gave them a musical rendition of 'Yes we have no bananas'. The Oregonians reckoned that I was a Limey who could 'put it on'.

"I eventually worked for the Portland bureau of parks and recreation. There was a programme of events to entertain a predominantly black clientele of which I had no previous experience. There was a visiting troubadour complete with mandolin, a visiting craft lady, and I found myself at one point trying to recover four-year-old Wayne's dentures from the paddling pool. At one time I saw a group of black men huddled together in a corner of the park at a picnic table. I watched them for a while to find out what they were doing. I discovered they were gambling and decided to put a stop to it. I went up and asked them to disperse and desist and one of them came up to me and said I had just put myself into trouble. Not deterred, and being naïve, I told them to go. The next day an American up a tree attracted my attention and introduced himself as FBI agent Ed Smith. He was staking out this gang who were serious, vicious and illegal gamblers. He told me he would deal with it, which eventually he did.

"It was an explosive time in the USA. Martin Luther King was on the march and flower power was sweeping San Francisco. In Peninsula Park, North West Portland, I organised a dance. It was very hot, the band was late and there was bad temper around. Eventually when the dance broke up there was a scream and all hell broke loose. The gates were locked by the authorities, who suspected a murder had been committed, and there was some panic. We discovered it was a false alarm and the scream came from a bunch of kids. There was tear gas, broken shop windows and press coverage. The headline was that it had been a 'teen age rumble'.

"When our time working in America was up, we headed home and we looked at the advertisements in *New Society* magazine. I applied successfully for the job of youth worker in Windsor – a job again dedicated to getting youth into church. This was a culture shock after Oregon and Birmingham. The chairman of the interviewing panel was Miss Gladys Hanbury-Williams who lived in a grace and favour residence in Windsor Castle. My remit consisted of basic youth activities such as table tennis, but I wanted to be more creative than that. Yehudi Menuhin was directing and performing at the newly established Windsor Festival and, with friends, I organised a fringe around it. We had Punch and Judy on Eton bridge, a Victorian magic lantern show from Brighton in the Guildhall (later of Charles and Camilla fame), and I wrote a mystery play based on traditional medieval lines called the *Play of Our Creation*.

"We performed this, by invitation, in St George's Chapel, Windsor, to which I had never been, but imagined it would be like any other sort of Methodist chapel. We were addressed by one of the canons who told us we must behave and if anyone wanted to use the toilet to remember it was the one used by the Duke of Edinburgh. Of course everyone wanted to be able to say they had used that particular toilet. During rehearsal the canon came up to me and said there was a couple misbehaving disgracefully behind the high altar. The play was a success and the canon very understanding. I had depicted God ascending into heaven by means of a giant stepladder. We featured Adam and Eve, Sin, Lazarus rising from the dead and dancers writhing on the floor in the Fall of mankind.

"We also put on a carol concert in Trinity parish church where I asked if they had a spare organ (thinking of a portable harmonium) and was firmly put in my place. They did not go in for such instruments there. The band of the Blues and Royals arrived in full uniform to provide the music.

"After Windsor I took a job in Birmingham at the Midlands Art Centre for Young People. However, I did not stay long as I found it difficult to get on well with the autocrats. So

Pat and I moved to Glasgow where I got a job in Bridgeton - the equivalent of London's East End - promoting community arts, learning the language, understanding the culture of the 'Orange' marches in this sectarian area, and meeting some lovely, and some not so lovely people. I also learned fire eating and practised this dangerous art at concerts for charity where we performed the 1812 Overture. I would blow paraffin into a torch and make an impressive flame at the right moments in the musical score. Pat did not encourage my fire eating. "I worked part time at Barlinnie gaol with its Class A prisoners, every one of whom was a murderer, and, together with a friend, Alistair Tyrie, made a clay exhibition of Tolkien's *The Hobbit.* I made wedding cakes. The first was for a prisoner who was marrying another inmate. I told him I needed money up front to make and decorate the cake. After his initial surprise he directed me, with his best man, to a well protected pub where I collected £200 in a brown envelope. I was advised to keep it well out of sight. I got other cake making commissions. At one wedding I was asked to play the piano as the guests were gathering. It took ages to start and I was told this was because they had forgotten to cook the tatties (potatoes) to go with the steak pie and beans, and we would have to wait. By this time I had seven glasses of whisky lined up on the piano. The ladies got into trouble for walking on the bowling green with their high heels.

"I had no formal training in making cakes but Mother always encouraged us to come into the kitchen at home when she was cooking. Father at one time worked in the kitchens at Holkham Hall. I learned to retrieve cake making disasters.

When our cat walked over the wet icing it had to be repaired at short notice. But the new royal icing would not set in time and the pillars of the multi-tiered cake started to tip and sink. Pieces of dowling were put under the pillars to hold them – a unique idea, I thought, until I learned that it was standard practice in the trade. I always used bright colours for my cake icing and this suited the functions in Glasgow. I did a flower festival and a Nigerian wedding, for example, when colour and show were essential.

"I stayed in my role of promoting art in Strathclyde until I retired. I have been playing a growing part in the local Episcopalian (Anglican) church, where I am rector's warden, and serve the chalice."

Peter and Pat have two children, Matthew and Jane. Matthew is aged 36 and manages a desktop publishing shop. He and his wife, Janet, have a son and a daughter, Neil and Abigail. Jane, aged 34, trained as a nursery nurse but prefers working in ASDA. She and her husband, Mark, have a son, Owen. They all live close to Peter and Pat in Glasgow.
Peter enjoys writing and is researching background on the use of samphire, first used in cooking in the 17th century. The samphire with which we are familiar in Norfolk is otherwise known as glasswort. There another variety known as rock samphire and that is mentioned in Shakespeare's *King Lear*.

Peter Beck

Peter Beck's family has lived in North Norfolk for generations. His father, Charlie, born in Walsingham, worked for Searle's grocery business in Burnham Market, and his mother, Kathleen, known as Cissy, was born in Burnham Overy. They first met at a dance. When war was declared Charlie was called up into the army and, apart from occasional leave, was away for the duration. Meantime, Cissy took over his job at Searle's delivering groceries in the district. They lived at West View, Burnham Market when Peter was born in 1935.

"I can remember the troops stationed in the village during the war. We had a lot of soldiers from the Welsh Regiment and their HQ was at the Rectory. Some of them married local girls. A Home Guard unit was formed. Concrete gun pads were built in Whiteways Road and two of them are still visible today. They were used by tanks and 25-pounder guns firing on targets on Scolt Head. Infantry trained on Holkham marshes. They did damage to the sand dunes and beach huts and these were never rebuilt after the war. Some of them were quite elaborate conversions: for example, one had been a pair of railway carriages, joined by a brick built chimney. It is still possible to find shrapnel and grenades in the sand as remnants of wartime destruction. "I started school at Burnham Market when I was five. One of my earliest wartime memories was a crashing American fighter plane. It came down where the pumping station stands at the corner of Friars Lane and Overy Road. The pilot had baled out and drifted down on his parachute into the meadow alongside our garden at West View, soon afterwards, unhurt. His plane was in trouble but he was blinded by the glare of the sun on the greenhouses, where Timmy Roy now has his nursery. I can remember when bombs were dropped near the railway station.

"At school I was mainly interested in maths, history and geography and of course football and cricket. I passed my eleven-plus in 1946 and went to Fakenham school by coach each day. The harsh winter of 1947 cut us off completely and there was no school for three weeks. Burnham Market was a self-sufficient village. There were Roy's and Everitt's mills for flour, bakeries, butchers, farms, blacksmiths, carpenters and other crafts. We could survive a siege. Employment was mostly agricultural with its accompanying services. Every Monday hundreds of cattle and sheep were herded through the streets to and from the stock pens where they were sold and shipped out by rail or returned to farms on the hoof for breeding stock.

"There were cattle pens at the railway station and behind the Hoste Arms. The auction took place on the Green. It was a fine sight to see animals being herded through the village on a Monday. There is a roadway between Station Road and the cattle pens at the station. The trains also took out sugar beet and other field crops and were the lifeline to the outside world. This went on until the early 1960s when the trains were discontinued and Burnham Market declined into a decade of limbo.

"Horses played a key part in deliveries until well after the war. They knew their way around, sometimes better than the driver, who might be otherwise occupied sleeping it off in the back of the cart. Charlie Wright, one of five butchers in Burnham Market at the time, had a pair of magnificent high-stepping horses which he used to pull his meat delivery cart. After a day's work he would turn them out into the orchards along the Overy Road. We asked him if we could ride them and he agreed, provided we could catch them. So we sat on the wall and as a horse came past one of us would leap over it and catch the horse by its mane. Once on, the horse would co-operate until it got fed up and would make for a low branch to shed the rider. These horses had probably been trained for dressage.

"I stayed at Fakenham school until I had taken my 'O' levels in 1951 and at the age of 16 joined the Royal Navy as an artificer apprentice on what was planned to be a 12-year engagement. The first two years were counted as 'Boy Service' outside the 12-year engagement. I started my four years as a naval apprentice at Torpoint in Cornwall to study general craftsmanship.

" At the end of my first year of apprenticeship I could choose my specialist trade and opted to become a shipwright and boat builder. After Torpoint I was drafted to HMS *Caledonia* at Rosyth. At the end of my apprenticeship I joined the Inshore Flotilla at Harwich consisting of inshore and coastal minesweepers, carrying out maintenance work on the wooden and aluminium hulls.

"In mid 1956 I was drafted to HMS *Narvik* to go to Christmas Island where a nuclear bomb was to be tested. However, the Suez invasion intervened, all drafts were stopped, and the Inshore Flotilla moved to Malta. Some minesweepers with divers aboard went on to the Canal to remove mines from sluices and sunken ships, but we came back to the UK before Christmas and were drafted to HMS *Diamond,* the destroyer that was to escort the Queen in HMY *Britannia* on her visit to Copenhagen. We also accompanied her on her review of the home fleet off Cromarty. We then went on to the Western Isles where the Queen spent her summer holiday in *Britannia*. Then we escorted HMS *Ark Royal* to Norfolk, Virginia, and celebrated the sailing of the *Mayflower* with a further fleet review, returning to the UK via Bermuda.

"The *Diamond* had been adopted by de Beers, the international diamond corporation, and she was granted the Freedom of the City when she berthed in the Pool of London where HMS *Belfast* is now permanently moored. This was a memorable week and we were entertained by de Beers and the City. Then by contrast we sailed for Birkenhead to test new propellers.

"They were fitted at night and the next day we set out to test their speed over a measured mile off the Isle of Arran, and then to Loch Goil to test their noise level which was designed to be very low to evade submarines. It was very deep with sharply sloping sides and as we sailed up and down, underwater noise trials were carried out. Then it was back to Birkenhead with the data and a repeat performance the next day with a new pair of propellers.

"When the trials were completed we sailed for dry dock in Chatham for a refit and were then drafted to a new ship in Glasgow, but they called us prematurely. The ship was not ready and there was nothing to do. We were asked where we wanted to go and I opted for HMS *Ganges* at Shotley near Ipswich, looking after boats used by the boys' training.

"In 1958, eight years into my 12-year engagement, I was approached to run the boathouse in Burnham Overy Staithe. Arthur Haines had left and it needed some new vigour. I weighed up the options. After eight years in the Royal Navy I was at my most valuable to them and would have to buy myself out of the remainder of my engagement. I had spent all my holidays and spare time at Overy with Billy Haines and then with his son Arthur, since I was 12, so I was very familiar with everything and I decided to take the opportunity. I came out of the Royal Navy at Easter 1959 and found so much had to be done.

"I slowly built it up, starting with boat repairs, renewing and supplying rigging and developing a specialist chandlery. It took 10 years to get it going and then it really went ahead. George Cleaver worked with me until he retired and then I was on my own.

"In 1959 I married Melba Cooper, born in Wells and who was a PE teacher at Dereham high school. We have three children. Julie, born 1962, is a nurse at the Norfolk and Norwich University Hospital. Mark, a naval architect, was born in 1964 and Paul, a PE teacher, was born in 1968. For 41 years I lived at the boathouse with the family and ran the business. In the year 2000 I reached the age of 65 but was looking forward to continued involvement. It was not to be. Fortunately we still owned the house in Burnham Market, where my parents had lived, and Mel and I moved in. The Holkham Estates made a barn available to me where I repair boats for many of the friends I have made over the decades.

"During my 41 years in Overy Staithe I experienced exceptional weather conditions: floods, severe storms, blizzards, very hot summers, for example 1976, and the extreme cold of January 1963 when the creek was frozen over and the ice was nine inches thick. I re-established the sailing club in 1960 and have been very much involved in that and the regatta with many sailing events along the north west Norfolk coast. I have always supported village life and have been a member of the Burnham Overy parish council."

Peter was presented, at a ceremony in Cromer, with the RNLI Award on Vellum in the late 1970s for rescuing children from a boat that got into trouble outside Scolt Head.

Peter Beck's wife Mel and their three children have been a constant support in this 'family business'. They were involved in all aspects of the general well being of the harbour and village. Their sons Mark and Paul participated fully until they went away to university or college. They manned safety boats and taught holiday-makers to sail and helped with the regattas. Visitors

Stern to bow Mark, Mel, Paul Peter

constantly sought Peter's advice on tides, the weather and helping to understand the elements. Mark and friends went on to design and build a 60ft steel boat at Overy Staithe when he left London University with his Master's degree, and sailed it round the world in 1993.

"Burnham Overy Staithe has changed a great deal over the years and not necessarily for the better. There are fewer locals living there and this has affected the atmosphere of the village. It has also suffered from congestion, typical of beautiful parts of the North Norfolk coast. The car problem is chicken and egg. The more car parking provided to ease congestion, the more cars come to fill the space and cause more congestion in the village and in the harbour. In years gone by Overy was a place which controlled itself. I sit on the Harbour Trust Committee which is trying to preserve the best while adjusting to car-borne realities. As everything becomes more commercial and developed, so the days when the village and the harbour ticked along with their own charm are receding into memory.

"People who wanted to come to Norfolk found their way here without the need for advertising. But now advertising promotes the beauty, peace and solitude of the North Norfolk coast and it is defeating those very benefits. An example is the Coastal Path, which I strongly opposed, because it would then be marked on the Ordnance Survey map. The opportunity to discover the wild and beautiful part of the coast for one's self would be spoiled by the 'magnet' of that line on the map. We shall have to work hard to preserve Overy.

Mike and Anne Cringle

Mike Cringle's family has lived in North Norfolk for generations.   Mainly seafarers, the names of his ancestors appear in old churchyards very close to the sea along the North Norfolk coast.   They feature also in old trade directories which list master mariners and the like.   Mike Cringle's book *The Gamekeeper's Boy,* published in 2000, establishes that the Cringles came originally from the Isle of Man and, in the 18th century, were doubtless engaged in the busy coastal trade that went on around the British Isles in those days.

In the mid 19th century, 100 years later, there were several Cringles still here and one of them was the famous Captain Cringle who became well known for having seen a sea serpent in mid Atlantic.   This was a confirmed sighting but news of it dogged him for the rest of his life, when he was doomed never to be free of someone asking him about it. *The Gamekeeper's Boy* is about Mike's father, Pat, who was born in Wells at the close of the 19th century and grew up there, full of enterprising activities connected with his beloved marshes, and assisting his grandfather, and other gamekeepers, on the Holkham estate.   In 1914, just before the outbreak of the First World War, Pat went to visit his brother who was farming in the USA. Pat served with distinction in the war, notably when he became responsible for an army bomb-making enterprise, uncomfortably close to the front line.

On his return from the war, Pat became a miller and businessman and worked for the government's War Agricultural Committee. In his later days he wrote articles for the *Shooting Times*. *The Gamekeeper's Boy* is a compelling account of life in remote North Norfolk in the first half of the 20th century. It is an evocative piece of Norfolk history told in Mike's inimitable style.

Mike has now written his autobiography, soon to be published and not to be missed. It is entitled *Norfolk, Nairobi and Elsewhere*. It starts when he was eight years old soon after the outbreak of the Second World War. Mike and his friend George gave full vent to their imagination in fanciful adventures, not least that they were crashed aircrew on the run from German invaders. Mike's ambition was to fly as soon as he was old enough to do so, and at the age of 18, for his national service, he volunteered for a four-year aircrew engagement.

This was not a great success, for though he did in fact learn to fly, he then finished off his four years on the ground. The job he found himself doing was 'personnel selection', which meant living and working amongst recruits and helping to sort them out for suitable RAF trades. It was not at all the sort of life he had envisaged when he volunteered, but was the fate, no doubt, of many a romantic young hopeful who saw himself as Biggles with a silk scarf blowing in the wind. At the end of four years he had had quite enough of all that and had to work out what to do next.

"I did not know what I wanted to do but a chance meeting, and some ads for posts overseas, beckoned me towards Kenya where the government was looking for suitable persons to work for them as administrative assistants on an initial two-year contract. It was not explained exactly what the job entailed, but it sounded vaguely Sanders of the River, and the pay was good; an attractive proposition for someone aged 22, unemployed after four years in the RAF, and looking for something interesting to do."

Mike lived in Kenya for 10 years, working firstly as an administrative assistant with the police, then with the Kenya Department of Agriculture. He moved into farming through a series of locum jobs.

"By the time of Kenya's independence 'Uhuru', I was running a farm that I had taken over from its previous owner who had decided to leave East Africa several years previously. It was in the Kipsigis area of western Kenya and many of them lived on 'my' land, working for me in a casual sort of way. With the coming of 'Uhuru', a local bigwig called Teita arap Towet became Minister of Agriculture, and he wanted to start a co-operative for his fellow Kipsigis. He approached me about buying up my land to be part of the co-operative, and we worked out a deal that would give me a reasonable profit, and would allow the local people who already lived on the farm to take it over.

"I was footloose and fancy free, also a tiny bit bored with managing several thousand lonely acres in the middle of Africa, and was quite happy to agree. I gave my breeding herd to the people who would take over, sold some of my stock for handy cash, and moved on. Most of the other Europeans in the area did much the same, and one or two stayed. There was none of the nasty anti-white land grabbing that went on in other parts of Africa."

In his book Mike describes the impact of the Mau Mau insurgency on the rural life of Kenya with a sang-froid that can best be described as character forming. He returned to Britain to start a new life in 1965.

His autobiography is a compelling book. It is written in a pacy, descriptive style, observant, interesting and very entertaining.

We now pick up his story from his return to the UK in 1965.

" Having nothing particular to do, but with a little money and a fair knowledge of farming, I decided I would go to Scotland and see if I could find myself a croft, which sounded interesting.

However, I had not found out then quite how bleak the climate was.

"I had been given the name of a lady in Glasgow who 'probably knew a lot about Scotland' and duly called on her one Sunday evening, having driven up from Wells where I was staying with my parents. Fate flipped an entirely unexpected card out of the pack at this point, because the Scottish lady was not at home and I was met at the door by Anne who rented a room there and was something to do with the art school."

Anne was born in Glasgow in 1936 and brought up there and in Ayrshire. She explains:

"My family traced its roots back for generations in the south of Scotland and was related to the Black Douglas. I was christened Anne Douglas Hunter. My father was an engineer, until the Depression, when he and my mother moved to Glasgow. He became a policeman and my mother the infant mistress at schools in the locality. My father's occupation meant that he had to stay put on the outbreak of war and I went to live with my grandmother at Patna, a small village on the banks of the River Doon deep in the heart of Robert Burns country."

Anne excelled at school, notably in the field of art and design, and trained as a teacher. She was headhunted, at the impressively early age of 21, to be a visiting lecturer at the Glasgow School of Art.

"They paid me well, by the hour, but only for the hours I worked. My father did not approve of this precarious source of income and determined that I should have a further source for the time I was not working at the college. He said as much to Harry Barnes, the deputy director of the Glasgow School of Art. Harry Barnes's daughter attended a boarding school in Helensburgh and the art mistress, Joan Tebbutt, needed an assistant.

"This led to my teaching two days a week at St Brides School in Helensburgh, where there were many ambassadors' children, and art was one of the subjects they could relate to. Joan encouraged them to go on to 'O' level and in many cases it was the only exam they passed.

"I taught some rough lads in Glasgow how to draw, in preparation for their chosen career in tailoring. They needed to develop an eye for clothes and style and I encouraged each of them to imagine they were designing for someone they would like to go out with. We got on very well and in return they offered to introduce me to Barrowland, Glasgow's equivalent of London's East End."

Anne's parents had moved to the north of Scotland and Joan Tebbutt, her fellow teacher at St Brides, offered Anne digs at her flat. It was there that this handsome young man, Mike Cringle, rang the doorbell on a Sunday evening when Joan happened to be out. Mike's call on Joan Tebbutt in search of advice to find himself a croft, found him a wife instead. The attraction between Anne and Mike was mutual and immediate and they married in mid July.

Mike continued, "By this time Anne and I had visited numerous crofts and farms around the UK and found that the only affordable land was poor land. The last straw was a dull, bleak, unlikely looking place, where a forest had been cut down, strewn with dead sheep on top of a mountain. We had high hopes on the way to it because we were following a car with the registration BUY. This turned out not to be a favourable portent and added to the anticlimax. We came to the conclusion that it was going to be difficult to combine the skills of a cattleman from Kenya with those of a design and embroidery expert from Scotland. So what should we do? My family had always been in business and were self employed – a rigorous discipline which makes one unemployable. Whatever it was, we wanted to do it together and we hit upon antique dealing for no particular reason.

"Although we did not know it at the time this was about the beginning of the antiques boom, that went on for many years, and the small business we started in Norfolk did well. We had decided to establish it in Burnham Market. The Old Black Horse pub, recently de-licensed by the brewery, was an attractive Grade II listed building, ideally suited to an antique shop – given that it could be brought up to condition from its rather neglected state. Nobody had spent any money on it for years and two floors were in such a desperate condition that you were in serious danger of falling through to the cellar below. Paint had not been used on it much either, and most of the walls were coated in a yellow brown residue of many years' tobacco smoke.

"We had a lot of help from my father, now at last retired, living nearby at Wells and available for many an odd job: and some quite major jobs. He even made some furniture for us. We discovered as time went on that as we cleaned and refurbished and got rid of some of the rather nasty 'modernisation', the old building was in what we had learned by now to call 'good original condition'.

"Plywood and plasterboard had covered old and interesting features like cupboards and fireplaces, cheap partitions had divided rooms, and a splendid attic room which ran the whole length of the house had superb oak beams and a 17th century window which had appeared from under piles of old plaster and rubbish.

"In addition to refurbishing the building we had another very important job to do which was to learn to be antique dealers. So we went to auctions and bought piles of books about old furniture, porcelain, antique glass, anything, in fact, to do with The Trade. We put a £5 limit, initially, on any one purchase and started to buy the odd item, which we usually found later turned out to be rubbish. These were the days when it was possible to buy a good chest for £20. We had the odd brush with The Ring; we were even invited to join them, but, apart from an instinctive reluctance to do so, feared that we could be getting into something that could turn out to be uncomfortable. So we remained doggedly independent. By the time we opened our shop in November 1965 we had begun to know a little about the rudiments of how it all worked.

"The week we opened it snowed - unusual for the Norfolk coast in November and probably the worst week of the year to open a new shop.   We took £30 that week which, although not a lot of money, at least showed we could buy and sell things, even in a snow storm.   One of our very first customers was Lady Margaret Douglas-Home, one of two dealers already in the village.   She and her friend Elizabeth Sumpter ran a very high-class business in the centre of the village.   The other dealer, Billy Williamson, had a sort of shed in North Street, less smart but still a very good and serious business.   This was good for us because it meant that a wide range of potential customers from all over the country, and especially from London, used to gravitate to Burnham Market.   Many a big dealer who would not otherwise have known of our existence would visit our very humble establishment having viewed Billy's general furniture and Lady Margaret's fine porcelain.

"Apart from this antique trade the village, judged by later years when it became a popular holiday resort, was very quiet in those days.   It looked exactly like one of those greyish black and white old photos you sometimes see.   Years earlier it had been a busy centre for the farming community around it, with blacksmiths and workshops and good old-fashioned ironmongers stores.   But it had declined steadily by the 1960s, and while there was still one of those old ironmongers, with a wonderful stock containing many items you couldn't even put a name to, there seemed to be no large scale business.

"There were a few local shops, post office, butcher, baker, a sweet shop, a good grocer plus a rather strange general store run by two ladies. It was a useful village centre but few came to it from very far away except two or three families who were rich enough to have a cottage that they used during the school holidays. Most days there were few cars in the village, the greens were un-kerbed and raggedy round the edges and there were few trees. I remember being told by someone, 'You shouldn't have bought that place in the village: the only worthwhile property is up Herrings Lane.' There is always someone to cheer you up but we started our business and had high hopes.

"Most of the fine trees that became a feature of the village centre were planted after we arrived. We looked out of our windows one morning and there were several people busy digging holes all over the grass and putting in saplings. It must have been one of the first moves to smarten up the village centre."

There was an established youth club for older children but none for the very young. In 1966 Anne was asked if she would start and help run a junior youth club and with Harry Farrow did so for 20 years. It used to occupy an upstairs room at the Hoste Arms and it was a great success, to the point where it sometimes threatened to come through the ceiling into the bar. The bar used only to be occupied by two or three old men in those days, who were not used to much excitement. Anne, who was more used to the street-wise kids of Glasgow, could hardly believe these countrified children so sheltered from the outside world, some of whom hardly ever left the village. She organised various outings such as a visit to the pantomime or picnics in the summer.

Then in 1975 Lady Margaret offered to raise some money for these treats by holding a craft fair on the greens. Anne, who said she would help to organise it, recounts the history:

"We set to work without further ado. Lady Margaret invited many of her friends to join in and Mike constructed a shelter for a very upmarket musical instrument maker out of a canvas boat cover. There were no other tents and gazebos as we see today, but it did not rain and the whole thing was sufficiently successful to resolve to do it again the following year. Thus, without any serious planning, began a tradition that has gone on year by year ever since, growing bigger and bigger and which has raised many thousands of pounds for youth organisations, and latterly also for the village school. Many people in the village have helped in running it in all sorts of ways, from planning the whole event to turning up on the day and helping with transport and parking. No doubt the visitors who come flocking into the village on craft fair day think it is some sort of ancient tradition that has gone on for ever. However, it was started 31 years ago by a good-hearted elderly lady and her young and slightly bemused assistants."

Anne

Anne's successful career as a lecturer at the Glasgow School of Art had come to a halt when she swapped an assured future in her field to join Mike as an antique dealer where there was no assured future at all. However, as the business developed successfully, she was able to apply her many talents to parallel activity. She took up her old career again as a sideline, designing and carrying out complicated collage pictures of interesting houses from cottages to castles. She soon had commissions from lots of people who fancied seeing their home as a work of art, framed and hung up on their sitting room wall. Many houses scattered throughout East Anglia must have one of Anne's 'house portraits' on their walls. One that must have been seen by many over the years is the collage she did for the Blakeney Hotel, showing the quay, the hotel and assorted shipping. It is still there, occupying most of the wall on the landing halfway up the main staircase. It is the biggest one she ever did and it was quite a performance getting it there on a large roof-rack and fixing it in position.

Anne also worked with architects and designed church panels and a pulpit fall in an explosion of colours depicting light and happiness for Easter for St Giles Cathedral in Edinburgh. "The Victoria & Albert Museum bought embroidery from me and I had an exhibit in Liberty's window at their Regent Street store in London and as part of the Embroiderers Guild exhibits in Glasgow and London. My work was shown in an exhibition at Hampton Court Palace.

"Eventually the demands on my time meant that I had to give up taking further commissions. Our children were growing up. We have two children: Frances (Frankie), born in 1968, and Tom, born in 1972. Frankie started her career as a graphic designer before moving on to work in sales and customer services. She is married to another graphic designer, and they have a son, Owen. Tom studied graphic design, did a spell in the building trade, went back to college to study architecture, and has now ended up as a full-time artist, selling his pictures of the coastal scene in art galleries in Burnham Market, Norwich, Aldeburgh and London. He is married to Suzanna, a barrister, and they have two children, Angus and Elizabeth. They all now live in Norfolk.

"Besides, we ran two shops by this time. In addition to the Black Horse we had bought the Standard House in Wells, specialising in pine furniture and old bottles which at the time sold for £7 to £9 each. Some enterprising lads from Southend had discovered a dump of them at Stiffkey and there was no shortage of supply.

" It was difficult to run two shops when the antique business is a very personal one between the client and the proprietor and it was impossible to be in two places at once. If Mike's customers wanted to see him they never knew where he would be when they called. Eventually we sold the Standard House to Charlie Ward. As Burnham Market was discovered by second-homers in the late 1970s, there was a demand for furniture, glass and porcelain and business went from strength to strength."

In 1978 Anne was appointed a magistrate on the Hunstanton bench and sat there and at King's Lynn on the family panel until Hunstanton moved all work to King's Lynn. Anne sat as a chairman for many years and eventually retired after 20 years. One of her enduring memories was sitting with a judge, hearing a case in the magistrates court – a situation she would never have presumed would be her privilege - a girl from Glasgow sitting with a judge in Norfolk.

"In the same year Mike and Anne joined the Bircham Jubilee Small-bore Rifle Club and Anne took up target rifle shooting as a hobby. "I became a good shot," says Anne, " represented Norfolk in county teams and became the women's county captain – a post I still hold. I also ran the open county shoots and became small-bore rifle secretary. Now I no longer shoot, nor run the open shoots, but am still involved with the administration of the sport in the county. Mike is the trophies officer for the county.

"Relaxation tended to centre on our boats. When the children were young many weekends were spent on our floating 'caravan', a 22ft Kestrel, and latterly on our Twinkle Ten. We always sailed at Wells and a lot of our time was spent at the East Hills – my idea of heaven.

Mike is a successful author.

"I used to write a monthly article for *The Paper* which circulated in the village for many years. The theme of my articles was based on stories about my father as a boy at the beginning of the 20th century. He had been quite well known as a writer for the *Shooting Times*, being an expert on wildfowling and the natural history of the Norfolk coast. These articles had only ever appeared in the *Shooting Times,* yet they were of interest to a wider readership. So I put some of these stories together with other material to make a book called *The Gamekeeper's Boy*. To my surprise this first book was accepted by a local publisher and has been in the bookshops ever since. I have now completed another book, much of which is the story of my 10 years in Africa. My earlier writings for the local newsletter consisted of accounts of what was going on in the village. This was useful as a member of the parish council to which I was first elected in 1991 and as its chairman for 10 years, as it gave a measure of continuity so issues did not get lost to memory between meetings.

"We had our share of excitements, usually because someone had an idea and wanted to make the village do something it did not want to do. My baptism of fire came when Westgate Hall, the big house at the end of the village, was up for sale and one or two people were convinced that we ought to buy it and make it into a grand new village hall plus social centre plus sports centre and everything else. At the time our then chairman Reg Baldry was taken ill and I had just been elected vice chairman. Horrified, I realised that I had been landed with a very tricky number and I was going to have to deal with the bitter arguments that immediately arose between those for and those against.

"My situation was made worse by the fact that I knew very little about it, except that a lot of money was going to be involved, and that the village as a whole wasn't really interested in the plan. It was also said, by those against it, that the building was not at all suitable. Those who had formulated the idea were well primed with reasons for, and I had to sit and listen to their arguments, which were often quite convincing. Those against it were less well organised, and the whole affair was becoming difficult, so I said that an official village meeting would have to be called to make sure that everyone knew what was going on. I was still busy reading up how to organise this when suddenly the Westgate Hall plan was dropped. I was never told precisely why but what a relief!

"A few years later a rather similar situation arose, again with a plan for a new village hall. This time it was to be a new building, very grand and very expensive, and all the old arguments for and against started up. Again there would be a lot of money involved, again the village as a whole didn't seem to want it. Again after a lot of argument and heated exchanges the whole affair died down.

"Another long running and often rather bad-tempered affair was the campaign for a large, official car park. It is still running. The fact is that as Burnham Market has become more and more popular as a holiday resort so car parking has become more and more of a problem. There is very limited parking space in the village, and there is only one field near enough to the village centre to be used as a car park. And the owners of this field will only allow it to be used if they can also develop it for housing: and that will not be allowed by the present planning regulations. This state of deadlock has been the same for years now, with endless discussions round and round.

" While these village conflicts have added a little interest to parish council affairs, the fact is that the useful work that goes on all the time is the regular day-to-day running of things. Some of these are useful triumphs, like the work that has been done successfully to preserve the greens against the encroachment of cars, and especially 4x4s that seem to regard village greens as their natural habitat. The appearance and style of the village centre has also been preserved over the years, and this does not happen automatically.

"Originally Anne and I ran a simple, straightforward antiques business, but in recent years this has changed a lot, partly due to the way the village has changed for everybody, and partly because the antique business no longer has the buzz it had when we started. A few years ago when the antique world was becoming less lively, we began to look at other things, and now we do a brisk business in greetings cards and local crafts, and we run an art gallery. Antiques too, but that is the dullest part of our dealing.

"Another string to our bow these days is the holiday cottage we run. This was originally a small stable block in the yard of the old pub, which had to be extensively restored. An expensive job, naturally, and to pay for itself it has been let as a holiday cottage for several years now. Its restoration was a remarkable job carried out by John Falvey as Dove Builders who worked his magic as an artist in brick and timber. It is a listed building and the work was closely monitored by the local conservation department, who declared themselves highly delighted with the way he had conserved and restored the building. It has been a great success as a rented holiday cottage; people seem to love its quaintness and slightly strange original features like beams with the bark still on.

Alan Utting

Alan Utting was born in Front Street, Burnham Market on 4th September 1939. The Second World War had broken out the day before but the two events were not connected. Alan's father, Ernest George Utting, known as Ernie, had come to Burnham Market in the 1920s and took up lodgings in Front Street. He worked for the ironmongers Reggie Utting (no relation) for some months. However, they did not get on and Ernie left to work at Curry's in Wisbech, to which he travelled each day on his motorbike for two or three years. Then he came back to set up his own business in radios and cycles in a wooden shed in North Street, until the war.

By then he had two children, Brian and Alan. The shop was closed down on the outbreak of war when Ernie joined the RAF. When he returned after the war he opened up a shop in Front Street near Julers Yard. Then in 1952 he opened shop on the Green and West Norfolk Radio was born. The business grew and soon was selling household goods as well as electrical items and cycles.

"One of his big regular tasks was to charge accumulators to power the radios of the day. Each accumulator was marked with the owner's name and some 150 would be wired up and charged each day, overnight. A large van was bought and put on the road and a daily round built up covering the surrounding villages on set days of the week. Harold Oldfield from Titchwell was the van roundsman who joined the shop in 1949 and stayed until 1966. His first van, he recalls, had a water temperature gauge built in on the top of the radiator and wooden spoked wheels. To prevent the gear lever continually jumping out of gear it was necessary to put a block of wood between it and the dashboard.

"Harold was paid on commission and loaded his van daily with a wide variety of household goods, taking on 100–150 gallons of paraffin into the inboard tank. This had a pipe running to the rear of the van and was fitted with a tap. At peak the van and shop sold 2000 gallons a week and storage was in five or six 500-gallon tanks located behind Gilly's shop on Overy Road. Paraffin sold at 10 or 11 pence per gallon.

"On several occasions during hard winters the van would get stuck in snowdrifts. When this happened legwork became the order of the day to keep customers supplied with the necessary ingredients of life. Many houses were still using paraffin for lighting and heating. At such times offers of a lift from a local tractor across fields were gladly accepted. None the less, many miles were covered on foot to look after customers' needs.

"Harold was very well liked with many a story to tell from his 17 years of service. He became a good friend to all who worked with him. It was said at the time that he had done everything except deliver a baby. He would be asked to change failed light bulbs on landings, mend punctures in cycle tyres and wellington boots, and fit new wicks to table lamps and oil stoves. Most of these services were done as a favour to his customers on his daily round when he made 40 to 60 calls a day.

"Harold also operated his weekly credit accounts. The customers would buy goods from him and pay two shillings or an agreed amount off the account each week when he called. When the outstanding balance was low enough further purchases would be made to top up the account. Some customers would keep weekly payments going for years with Harold regulating the buying to paying ratio. They were hard times for some and quite often when the weekly call came round they would not answer the door, hence no two shillings that week.

Ernie acquired a smaller van for local work and during the football season he would also use this to do a Saturday night paper round, delivering bundles of 'Pink-Un' newspapers (football results and comments).

"When the USAF were at Sculthorpe, and renting houses in the area, they became good customers for paraffin, many taking 20-40 gallons per week to heat their homes which they liked to keep warm. A contract was signed in the mid 1950s at the base to supply black and white TV sets and a workshop and office were available on the base. The customers were encouraged to come to Ernie for the TVs and aerials which were installed on the base and in the rented houses from Hunstanton to Cromer. Payment was in dollars which could be exchanged for £ sterling in the base office, less their commission.

Over the next few years several hundred sets were rented in this manner, eventually being collected and stored in a garage behind the Hoste pub. Disposal of these old TVs was then a problem. However, Eddie King, the shop's electrician, came up with an idea. A friend of his was a driver for a scrap metal merchant in the Fakenham area, and Eddie told him that the storage garage was full of old washing machines, containing lots of scrap metal, and the odd TV set. On inspection the driver saw several old washing machines piled inside the door. They had been strategically placed and he agreed to collect the lot, good and bad.

"On the collection day the driver moaned about the load being mostly old TVs and not as much scrap metal as he had hoped. However, as agreed, he filled his lorry to capacity and left. Some weeks later Eddie asked his driver friend where they had disposed of the load and was told that it was nearly all still on the lorry as his governor did not know what to do with some 200 old TV sets. I wonder if they are still on that lorry today.

"The Queen's coronation was a major event in early television. A nine-inch GEC black and white TV was installed in St Edmund's Hall in North Street together with a massive aerial erected to receive pictures from the London transmitter. Some 150 people crammed into the small hall for this exciting event. The reception was very poor and the picture was full of snow, yet occasionally definite movement could be seen and everyone enjoyed the spectacle.

1977

"One Saturday afternoon the Queen Mother visited her friend Lady Margaret Douglas-Home who lived next door to the shop. Goods displayed outside the shop included a watering can, and one of the royal party came in and purchased it for use at Sandringham. The next day a telephone call was received from 'high up' thanking the shop for supplying it. By this time Ernie had another shop in Swaffham and three vans on the road."

"I went to Burnham Market school and after eleven-plus in 1950 I moved on to board at Wymondham College, where parents paid fees according to their income, and which was just emerging from its wartime role as a US forces base and then as a hospital. As it was, the Nissen huts were still there and were the main accommodation for the school. It was a big co-ed school with some 850 pupils and I spent five exciting years there gaining my GCEs. I did not, however, stay on for the sixth form.

"My brother Brian was by this time running the Swaffham shop for Ernie. When he left college he had come into the business, helping out at both Burnham and Swaffham shops. Brian was then called up to do his national service and signed on for three years in the RAF, the last two being in Hong Kong. When my turn for national service approached, I applied for deferment until Brian had completed his service. He returned in 1959 and I was already packed and raring to go when I received a letter to say that conscription had been abolished.

"On the introduction of VAT an inspector called on Ernie and asked to see evidence of stock held which would now be subject to VAT. When Ernie told him no stock inventory had been made the inspector told him he would have to carry out a full audit, to which Ernie replied, in so many words, 'If you want a stock check you can do it yourself.' A mutual agreement was eventually reached."

Ernie and Alan, father and son, did not see eye to eye. "We worked six days a week, usually ending up for a drink at the Old Black Horse pub on the Green at about 10.00 p.m. At the time we lived above the Swaffham shop and my mother seemed happy provided we were home by midnight. So after a few drinks it was down to me to meet the midnight deadline. My father would fall asleep by the time we reached North Creake and I had to drive like mad to make the deadline at Swaffham."

Ernie Utting thoroughly enjoyed his role of service to the village. He was very good with people, and had particular sympathy for old people, who found it difficult to cope. He took the view that we would all grow old one day and might need help ourselves. Quite often a service or small repair would be carried out free of charge for that 'poor old lady'. After a time it became evident to Alan that he had little interest in the commercial reality of the business but he was fulfilled in providing a service for everyone, particularly the elderly and single pensioners living on limited incomes. So after trying unsuccessfully to change this habit Alan moved out in 1959 and took a job in Enfield, Middlesex.

"In 1962 I became a service engineer for Radio Rentals and three years on I was appointed manager of the Kilburn branch in London. I had responsibility for some 3000 subscribers covering NW6, NW8 and W9 where there were largely Jewish and Irish communities.

"I can remember when cricket was being played at Lord's, our engineers had to service in pairs. One engineer would drop his mate off to repair a TV in a block of flats and, as no parking was permitted locally, the driver had to keep cruising around the area waiting for call completion and pick-up for the next call.

"Now married, I made an attempt to buy a house, but London prices made me apply for a branch transfer to the East Anglia area. Eventually I was offered and took over a busy Ipswich branch which I ran for four years, having found the house we wanted without difficulty. We used to holiday in Norfolk, calling on my parents when in the area.

In 1976 my wife Joan and I were was on holiday at Wells-next-the-Sea during that hot summer and visited my parents on our way back to Ipswich.

" My father looked tired and I said if he was thinking of selling the business I would like first option to buy it. To my surprise he told me I could have the bloody keys tomorrow. By September 1ˢᵗ we had made all the arrangements and I took over.

"The business was built on service but was not followed up with appropriate invoicing and cash collection. We had a mobile shop on the road, making 50 to 60 calls on customers' homes a day, and selling a wide range of goods from Aerial washing powder to Zebrite black grate polish. Times were changing fast and the van driver, now Denny Rix, was under pressure to make the rounds pay. While it secured the goodwill and customer loyalty it cannot be said to have been a profitable part of the business. When Denny Rix retired three years later in 1979 the van was taken off the road. I ran down the TV side, which was labour intensive, and concentrated on everyday goods. The range of goods we sold was changing all the time.

"One Christmas, in the early 1980s, with the help of Eddie King, we hung a few strings of coloured lights in the tree opposite our shop. This was very effective and the custom was taken up through the village in subsequent years until today it is a major feature every Christmas. Switching on the lights has become an event accompanied by mulled wine, mince pies and the arrival of Father Christmas.

"The shop clientele has changed with the 'discovery' of Burnham Market for its holiday and second home potential.

This has led to some considerable changes to the shop. Our son Richard carried out a survey one Saturday afternoon, counting the number of passers by who entered the shop. Over 50 per cent did not. At the time the front of the shop reflected the business of household goods. Holiday-makers were more interested in giftware and not looking for galvanised buckets and bars of soap. Changes had to be made to lure them in.

"Joan and our daughter-in-law Wendy had started a partnership together and were selling pine furniture and giftware products. Their business took off and they saw the logic of filling the front of the shop with tempting buys to encourage the other 50 per cent to take a closer look. Once this was done a further survey confirmed that 70-80 per cent came in to look.

"The success of the gift shop and fancy goods separation from household goods encouraged Joan and Wendy to expand that part of the business and set up a separate enterprise. This is W&J Utting and they now have shops in East Rudham, Holt and Snettisham where they have taken over a large complex and sub-let some of the shop space, making it into 10 units rented to various trades. In 2006 W&J Utting won the 'Young Business of the Year Award' given by the West Norfolk council.

"We have extended out at the back of the shop and expanded our range of household goods. We found that many of the additional passers by, attracted by the display of gifts and fancy goods at the front, wander through into the household section at the back to discover and buy items they had been unable to get elsewhere or had forgotten all about. It was an expensive project, costing over £90,000, but has given the business a new lease of life.

"We had an unexpected interruption to the excavations at the back when a skeleton was discovered by workmen digging under a wall. We contacted the building inspector who in turn sent for a professor of archaeology who identified the skeleton as Roman and not the remains of a difficult customer. We subsequently gave the skeleton a decent burial."

The other thing Alan reluctantly had to change was the shop name from West Norfolk Radio to Uttings. This became necessary because soon after the North Norfolk radio station was established, he started receiving telephone calls requesting a piece of music be played on our radio station for Uncle Bill in King's Lynn. They were advised that West Norfolk Radio was not a radio station but a shop. "I could see the logic in their calls so the name change had to take place.

"All too soon I find myself the wrong side of 65, and my daughter Victoria is slowly taking over the running of the business. I hope her next 30 years give her as much pleasure and job satisfaction as my 30 years have done. With that expectation I will gladly stand aside and wish her well with all my love and thanks."

Ron Cleaver

In 1978 Ron Cleaver's parents George and Ivy celebrated their golden wedding. Both were born in Burnham Overy Staithe. They had married in 1928 when George completed his career at sea with the Aberdeen White Star and the Shaw Savill lines. His first ship, the *Diogenes*, had two other Burnham men in her crew – Billy Scoles and Dick Barnes. George Cleaver then worked on Overy creek until his retirement in 1970, with Billy Haines, Arthur Haines and Peter Beck at the Burnham Overy boathouse.

George's father was killed in the First World War and his grandfather, Ron's great grandfather, was the skipper of one of the last sailing ships to use Overy harbour. At one time it handled 50–60-tonne coal ships and was a very busy place.

Ron Cleaver was born in Burnham Overy Staithe in 1938. There were five children: Ron, Bill and Len, Jill and Shirley.

"There were many well known characters in Overy Staithe as I grew up there. For example, the owner of the Overy Staithe village shop and post office, Jimmy Riches, who died aged 89 in 1960, was the last of his family to own the shop over many generations. He was the second youngest of 17 children. He told stories, handed down by old men, who remembered Nelson strolling along by the harbour during his years 'on the beach" waiting for a command.

"Before Riches village shop was demolished in 1970, there had long been rumours that a considerable amount of coin had been dropped by customers in the shop over the years and that it was still there. Coins had fallen between the floorboards and had not been recovered. When the shop was demolished to prepare the site for a new house to be built by Jimmy Riches' son Bertram, 10 years after Jimmy died, the rumours proved to be at least partially true. Coins were found and one of these was a silver fourpenny piece which went out of circulation in 1856. Also there were a number of foreign coins reflecting the international cross-section of the customers.

"Another well known character was George Phillips whose family had established the Moorings Hotel in 1926. He managed it later, for many years with his wife Muriel. There were distinguished regulars among the guests, some of whom found a house in the area and used it as a second home. George Phillips had a gallant war in the Royal Navy, became a lieutenant commander, won the DSC at Dieppe and was twice mentioned in despatches. His wife, Muriel, was honoured by Pope John Paul II with a special medal for her work for the Catholic church and not least, with her husband, for building St Henry's church in Burnham Market.

"The Phillips had a very large collection of stuffed birds at the Moorings and his aviaries had many colourful foreign species."

The combination of George Phillips' cooking and Muriel's untiring presence made it unique at the time. There were not many exceptional eating places in East Anglia. However, the Moorings was included in the first *Good Food Guide* produced by Raymond Postgate in 1956. Nevertheless, as late as 1980 the *Egon Ronay Guide* book was hard pressed to find more than a handful which he could describe as 'above average'.

"The pools and creeks at Overy Staithe were ideal for catching flatfish with a butt fork. This was a four-tined trident with which we speared them at low tide. Each tine had a fluke on it to prevent the fish wriggling off. I asked the blacksmith in Burnham Market, Jack Thompson, whose workshop was behind Satchells, to make one for me. This was a very effective way of catching fish – it called for the minimum of tackle and required no bait, but it could be hazardous with sudden holes in the pools at low tide."

Ron went to Overy school until the age of 10. He then, as many did, transferred to Burnham Market school which was situated on the site occupied by Oliver Lamps after the school was rebuilt in Friar Lane.

"My passion was football which I continued to play long after I left school. In fact I didn't give it up until I was 43, playing for Burnham Overy Staithe, then Burnham Market and

Burnham Thorpe. The headmaster of the school at the time was Mr Evans and I was also taught by Mrs Evans and Miss Rout.

" I left school in 1953, coronation year. There were only three TV sets in the village at the time and Arthur Mason owned one of them. The coronation launched television ownership, opening up the world to us, and television sets became much more of a household feature from then on.

"I took a job at Arthur Mason's garage to learn necessary engineering skills, although I was never formally indentured as an apprentice. When Arthur Mason thought I was ready to do the job unsupervised, I was expected to get on with it. He was a dealer with a bulging wallet, and was involved in a number of businesses including fairground organs and steam engines. He was obviously successful for he left a good business when he died.

"He had bought the site on the Creake Road when the Alley's three-way tipper trailer factory closed in the late 1940s and it is where Burnham Motors is today. I started my working career at Overy Staithe for four years and then on to this site in 1957 and have worked here, under some changing circumstances, for nearly 50 years – a total of over 53 years in the business.

"I had been at school with Mavis Fowle who came from Wighton, and we started courting when we were both 18. We eventually got married at the age of 24 and not before Mavis had asked the question many times if we intended to do so. We needed a house but I lived in a caravan adjacent to the garage site and near to the allotments of which there were many more then than there are today.

" After seven years I saw a bungalow, built by Fisches and for sale at £4500.   I went along to negotiate this and the insurance needed and could have bought it for £4250.   The salesman said I could not be doing a wiser thing, it was just right for me, etc.... until he asked me how much I was earning, which was £17 a week plus all the overtime available. He said I would have to be earning at least £30 per week plus overtime to afford this bungalow and I had better go and see Arthur Mason and talk to him.

"Arthur Mason said this was impossible but I needed a bungalow for a wife.   I said he felt the same way as Mavis. He did hint that he would let us have a piece of land for the cost of a week's wages.   This sounded like a good offer but we had to build a home on it.   Eventually he kept his word about the piece of land and we were on at least the first rung of the ladder. I was offered money for our caravan, to be paid when we eventually moved out of it.   However, Arthur Mason calculated we would make £100 profit on it and that profit was his. We had no contract for the caravan or the land except a handshake from Arthur Mason and by this time we had the bungalow shell built.   For two years I left work each evening and laboured on the house until 10.00 p.m. Eventually we moved in 1970.

There was a busy supply business to the beach huts and house boats at Scolt Head, overlooking the North Sea, but separated from Overy Staithe at high tide and quite a wet journey at low tide. This was a favourite destination for the owners of these beach huts in the holidays and weekends in the summer. There was a thriving supply business operated by Billy Haines and his family and by Welcome Thompson.

"Arthur Mason provided some US army surplus vehicles to drive in that challenging terrain to serve the beach house community. Among these was a DUKW which I can remember, when I was 16 or 17, delivering gas around the village. Then there was the Weasel, which was very uncomfortable, with its tracks like a tank, and a Muskrat, which had no reverse gear.

"In 1953 I and a group of friends were at the cinema at Wells when an announcement was made that the show had to stop and we should get home as quickly as possible as there was a terrible storm and the sea was flooding in. We made our way home with great difficulty. The sea wall defences had been breached and Roy's Mill was cut off. The railway line and much of the road was inundated and parts of the coast already cut off.

"The floods put paid to the railway line between Burnham Market and Wells and it was never to reopen. The line from Burnham Market to Heacham continued until about 1963 for freight, and then that closed. This changed the nature of Burnham Market. At one time it handled 1000 head of cattle on a Monday and 800 on a Wednesday on the site behind the Hoste Arms and most of the cattle were shipped in and out by rail.

"It also increased the number of road vehicles and after a difficult time of transition from agricultural employment the North Norfolk coast picked up as a holiday venue and with a growing number of second homes. Some of the owners of these did more for the local economy than others. There was a demand for craftsmen and services from those who chose to support the local community. Others did not want to know and bought their services from outside the area.

"When Arthur Mason died he left the garage business to his five daughters. I agreed to carry on and manage it for them. However, shortly afterwards his family decided to take their money out of the business, realise all the assets and sell it. This put its viability in jeopardy. For the next two years we were on a hand to mouth existence. Then John Rosser of Burnham Norton, who owns Gillies shop, became interested and bought the Masons' business. Steve Hood took out a lease to run it and keep the staff. I am responsible for the

Left to right: Bob, Ron, Keith, Kevin, Scott

workshop and have been the MOT director for 14 years. We have a good team and I have worked with Keith Kēster and Kevin Hewitt for over 25 years. We also have two apprentices, Scott and Bob, who are working for their qualifications."

Burnham Motors seems to be able to turn its skills to any sort of vehicle. There is an obliging, can-do attitude which is reminiscent of garages in days gone by. It has that reassuring oily, rubbery smell – music in the background and assorted calendars on the walls where each month gives way to another revelation.

Steve has built up the shop so it has become an amenity and not only for motorists.

"Mavis and friends, known as the Burnham Players, have put on variety shows for some years each November. This started in Burnham Thorpe and now takes place in Burnham Market. It includes singing and sketches and a bit of Norfolk humour. This has become a popular annual event. She is a keen supporter and season ticket holder of Norwich City football club. She is also steward of the Methodist chapel in Station Road.

"I have accumulated cups and medal over the years for football, bowls, darts and crib and spend spare time woodworking when I can. I have a double garage at home which is my workshop and have built a summer house, two wishing wells and a windmill. I have also built climbing frames over gateways and am in the middle of a project to build a car trailer.

"Each year in July we dress floats for the horticultural show and add to the excitement of the procession from the Market Place to the playing fields. My brother Bill won the Cup for 20 years in succession with produce grown on his double allotment in Burnham Market. At one time the show was the highlight of the year with fancy dress competitions and sports. It has recently been going from strength to strength and needs and deserves support from the village as a whole."

Ron and Mavis's daughter Sheridan lives in South Creake and has four children.

Cromer and Sheringham

Larry Randall

In 1881 Robert Laurence Randall moved to Cromer from Holt. He was one of two sons of William Randall who, earlier in the century, had built the gas works in Holt and opened a shop where he sold and repaired watches and clocks, gas appliances and services and bicycles. The business in Holt was not big enough for two sons to make a living. This was history repeating itself for in the 1860s when there were six boys and two girls in the family there had to be a dispersal and two of the boys emigrated to Fiji and New Zealand.

Now, a generation later, Robert moved to Cromer to set up there, leaving his brother to run the Holt business. Cromer was an expanding town, electricity was still to come and Robert set up a business similar to the one he had learned in Holt, initially in Chesterfield Villas, operating from his home. He then moved to Bond Street and later to Mount Street in about 1890 where he and his family lived above the shop.

In his first week of trading in Cromer he took one shilling and sixpence and paid out one shilling and sixpence. He would cycle around Cromer to reach his customers. When electricity first came to Cromer in 1906 the business expanded to install and service electric appliances. Electricity came to Sheringham for the first time in 1926.

He was a notable and respected citizen dedicated to the social good of the town where he started a branch of the Rechabites – very strict about personal conduct – no smoking, drinking or swearing - and the St John's Ambulance which operated out of the Mount Street shop. In a medical emergency Robert would instruct one of his staff to go and deal with it. In effect the ambulance service in Cromer was funded by the Randall business for many years. When Robert was wearing his St John's Ambulance uniform he would salute people in the town.

Robert had five sons, all of whom served in the First World War and, miraculously, survived. Harold served with the RAF in Germany, Reg served in Egypt and spoke Arabic and French on his return. Raymond, Larry's father, volunteered for Kitchener's army, served in the 10th Essex regiment in France and fought at the battle of the Somme where he was wounded in the leg at Delville Woods. He was repatriated to Liverpool and then back to Cromer to Colne House. Theodore served at Gallipoli with the Norfolk regiment. Robert also had three daughters – Mabel and Enid who became teachers in London and Sybil who became a nurse.

Once again the business had to divide to enable the family to make a living and this resulted in five Randall shops in

Cromer and Sheringham after the First World War. The eldest son, Wilfred, had become a teacher and moved to London. Theodore ran the watch making business and if he rolled up his sleeve there would be watches all up his arm while he tested them for time keeping. He later became captain of football at Cromer and played for Norfolk. Reg had a toy shop and hung a notice above the door saying that three languages were spoken inside – English, French and Arabic, although how much Arabic was in demand in Sheringham at the time is not recorded.

Robert Laurence Randall was a great educationalist with strong Methodist values. Advancing health care and better infant survival rate meant that many more members of large families survived to adulthood. As education and awareness of the opportunities available to young people developed, the next generation would question whether there could be fulfilment staying close to home. There was a demand for teachers and nurses and later for admin and clerical management. These were all factors in wider dispersal of families, in many cases across the globe.

None the less, the descendants of Robert Randall have held together well, still speaking to each other, and able to muster 30 to 40 close relations at family gatherings. Their family beach hut on the Cromer promenade has often been the venue for reunions.

Larry was born in April 1932 as one of two children of Raymond and May (née Wills). The other was his sister Dorothea.

"I went to school in Cromer and when I left in 1947 my father said he wanted to give me the chance he never had. I was to be apprenticed to Laurence Scott, the well known electric motor manufacturer in Norwich. I started my five-year engineering apprenticeship in the coldest winter in living memory. After one week the county was covered in a blanket of snow – six feet deep in places. It went on for a month and it was impossible to move around. We were effectively cut off in Cromer.

"At the end of my second year on the shop floor, I was transferred to the planning office to learn to be a planning engineer. When my time approached for national service I was told by Mr Gordon Brooks, my boss, that the firm would like to take me back when I had completed it. However, for the next month I must get out my tool kit and return to the shop floor, leaving the planning office.

" The implications of this were that I would be classified on my return in the job I had been doing at the time of leaving. This was a transparent ploy to offer my job back on lesser terms and I would have none of it. I demanded to see Mr Lee, the top man, whom I knew and respected. As I made for his office Mr Brooks protested that I could not just go barging in to see him. I told him to 'watch my smoke'.

"I introduced myself and Mr Lee said he knew me. I asked him if he would take a lesser job before going off for national service for the purpose of reducing the level of re-employment. He agreed that this was unreasonable and cancelled the arrangement. So I came back two years later to pick up where I had left off in the planning office.

"I joined the Royal Navy in 1953. There were 21 of us at the Colgate interview and I was accepted immediately. I don't know what happened to the other 20! After Southsea barracks ratings training, I took my trade test and passed. After fire control training I was posted to HMS *Royal Arthur*. I was promoted to the rank of petty officer artificer and took part in the 1954 fleet review. It was the best two years of my life. It not only gave me satisfaction but made a man of me.

"Before I went into my national service, HMS *Crossbow* visited Cromer in 1950, and we all had the opportunity to go around the ship which we reached by the local crab boat. This was the prelude. My second trip to HMS *Crossbow* was my posting to it on completion of my training. We went up to Norway into the fjords on submarine hunting exercises in conjunction with the RAF. We also visited Northern Ireland, Malta and Tangier before returning to Portsmouth.

"In 1955 I came out of the Royal Navy and resumed as a planning engineer at Laurence Scott where I stayed until 1976. There was then a call for volunteers to take redundancy. I volunteered on the basis that my family business needed me. My father was the only partner in the business and was ailing. Furthermore, if I left Laurence Scott that made one less who had to be made redundant.

"We had a manager of the shop in Mount Street and two skilled electricians in Bernard Moy and Eric Green who had been with the firm for many years. We were busy and getting busier and employed three apprentices. We have never looked back. The only shop we own, as opposed to rent, is 21 Mount Street, Cromer.

"One of my early expansion projects came when I tendered for the electrical work in 54 new houses being built by the district council. I proposed a novel deal, which they were pleased to accept. This was that they would buy and store the materials and I would do the installation work at the cost price I quoted on contract.

"We had a busy, hectic life in the business and one Christmas after a family meal, Richard Leeds said during a discussion about retirement, 'Think of me.' I had no immediate family to whom to pass the business. Richard is my second cousin and I was pleased to have the opportunity to hand over the business to the fourth generation.

"His grandfather Theodore and my father Ray were brothers. Theodore's daughter is Richard's mother. He is in charge of the business where he continues to apply the principle of care and respect to all of the customers. We do not make a charge for stepping over the threshold. I do not think it fair on customers to charge them a call-out fee regardless of what service (if any) they get. We have built our business on trust and reputation. This was an important move for me and the business.

" I became involved in the town council from 1976 and the North Norfolk district council, to which I was first elected in 1991 when I was also running the business.

"I had always been an Independent, politically, although I voted and supported the Conservatives. However, with a business in the town it is not advisable to flaunt a party political ticket, whatever it is. So when elected to the North Norfolk district council as an Independent candidate I and another five newly elected councillors formed a group known as the Conservative and Independent Alliance. This put the Conservatives and Alliance in power. We had 24 members compared to 22 for all other parties combined.

"I had been told that the only way to get on in the council was to join a group, so this was my response and I was soon elected to two key committees - tourism and leisure, and health and works." Cromer has been a substantial beneficiary of Larry's unceasing efforts on behalf of the town. He is known as Mr Fixit.

"I have time for everyone with a problem or who wants advice, whatever their political persuasion, whether they voted for me or not. It was often a case that, 'If you have a problem – ring Larry Randall. He will most likely be able to help you.'

"As a councillor my first duty is to represent the people of Cromer. I am a freemason and a Rotarian whose objectives I share – 'Service before self.' There are some who call me

'Mr Cromer', but that title belongs to Dr Donald Vaughn who was far more deserving.

"Donald Vaughn was the doctor in the town from 1923 until he died in 1992. Also known affectionately as Donald Duck, he had a narrow escape during the war. German planes were likely to drop any remaining bombs on us as they turned for home after an air raid. One time they directed their load on to the local laundry, which was near Dr Vaughn's house. It received a direct hit but Donald Vaughn and his wife were both out. Regrettably two builders were working there at the time and they were both killed.

"In 1997 I was elected to the county council as a Conservative. The county is a much more political body than the North Norfolk district council. I was put on four key committees – fire, museum, libraries and sea fisheries. This has been compatible with my continued work on the district council, which included planning."

Larry earned an enviable reputation for his work on the county council. Not only did this apply to the voters who had elected him but to that shrewd and knowing group of people – the staff at the council offices. "Larry was always on time, he had read his brief and was dedicated to the people of Cromer whom he served with dedicated purpose. He was never too busy to pass the time of day and take an interest in one's problems. Larry was a most reliable member of the council."

This is praise indeed when councillors and, for that matter, most people in public life, fall into two categories – those who want to BE something and those who want to DO something. "The difference is not hard to spot."

Larry has never flinched from controversial support for Cromer and those he represents. A good example is the traffic management scheme, designed to cut congestion in the town – particularly in the summer - but which had sparked protests from local fire, police and ambulance officers, doctors and residents. He called for engineers to take a fresh look at the plans. The *North Norfolk News* reported Larry's objections to the scheme in March 1999 thus:

' *Councillor Randall said the scheme was being pushed through too quickly and that consultees had not been given enough time to respond. He was concerned for those living in the areas affected and feared old people would not be able to get used to the scheme. "I support the people of this town and the public are not happy with it."*
The project engineer for traffic strategy at county hall said the work could not proceed without Councillor Randall's approval.

"In 2002 I was feeling unwell as Christmas approached but the staff Christmas dinner was scheduled to be held next day at County Hall. There was no way I was going to miss that but my condition got progressively worse and after lunch I confessed to not feeling too good. They suggested I should go to hospital straight away but I did not want to do that. They might never have let me out again. I drove home and called in at the doctor's surgery who gave me a very severe lecture diagnosing that I had suffered a mild stroke and should not have been at a Christmas lunch – let alone driving to and from the function.

"I demanded a scan, which the doctor said was unnecessary as it was obvious to him that I had had a stroke. However, I wanted to know if there was anything left of me up there. My right arm and hand had no feeling and my right leg was almost wholly numb. However, I was told that the condition would improve somewhat and so it has. My arm still has no feeling in it but I can walk and get on with life with minimal handicap.

"I am a member of Normit – Norfolk Major Incident Team - but I have given up much of my committee work. At 73 I reckon it is time to ease back a bit. I still play indoor and outdoor bowls and have continued interests in music and reading. I belonged for many years to the Norfolk Operatic Players and took part in productions at the Theatre Royal, Norwich, and other venues, of productions from *Nabucco* to *Annie Get Your Gun*, to Gilbert and Sullivan and much else besides."

Larry and his wife Mags still live in the house in Cromer where Larry was born and has lived all his life. Mags enjoys flower arranging and was one of the team representing North Norfolk to arrange flowers at Sandringham for the Queen's golden jubilee. She is a former chairman of the Cromer flower club which took her many times to both cathedrals in Norwich, big occasions throughout the county and as far afield as Jersey.

Larry and Mags

"We are a large family, with many cousins, and have a hut on the promenade where we meet up for special occasions. Thinking back to my grandfather, the committed Rechabite, I would not have qualified on any of the three criteria – non smoking, non drinking and non swearing.   I used to smoke 60 cigarettes a day but gave it up through determination of mind over matter.   My doctor said I had missed a trick because I could have raised a lot of money through sponsorship. As it is, I have not smoked for six years - and I don't drink much either.   But as to swearing…..!

"I believe we should make every day exciting.   As one wakes up in the morning there are certain things we can take for granted – the air, the sea, the birds, the flowers.   But there is much we do not know about the outcome of the day and we can influence that if we try – if only by responding positively to whatever it brings.

Brian Farrow

Brian Farrow was born in Sheringham in 1945. His father was born in Sheringham, one of a family of five, and was a professional soldier. His mother, one of seven children, was born in Happisburgh, the daughter of Tom Lawson who was born in Sheringham but moved to Happisburgh as a young man and was the last coxswain of the Happisburgh offshore rowing and sailing lifeboat in 1926.

"My family on both sides are steeped in the traditions of the fishing fraternity, some of whom were lifeboatmen. In the old days not only did lifeboatmen have the courage to face every mood of the sea but they had the additional hazard of leather thigh boots. If these became waterlogged it would send them straight to the sea bottom with no hope of rescue. Little wonder they gravitated to a coxswain who had the skills to get them home.

"North Norfolk coxswains have maintained their reputation and some, like Henry Blogg, have achieved universal fame for their work in the North Sea which old-timers called the German Sea.

"My father was invalided out of the army in the middle of the war and was unable to work for a very long time. The desperate situation saw the best of Norfolk family support in that both sides of the family rallied round – it was the only support available at the time and for a long while after that. As he recovered he tried his hand at anything, including labouring and that fall-back in the country in hard times, poaching. He owned a greyhound which often provided the odd rabbit or hare.

"After I passed my eleven-plus I went to board at Wymondham College which is a state boarding school. Most of my contemporaries went elsewhere, including Paston College, but Wymondham suited me well. It was a huge co-ed with 1000 boys and girls and had been established on a site of Nissen huts which had been an American army camp during the war and later a hospital. It was in effect a technical grammar school. I passed 11 'O' levels, 10 of them in technical subjects, and two 'A' levels. Boarding was in itself an adventure and the school gave me good opportunities for sport, notably rugby, cricket, fencing and athletics. Above all it gave me social confidence and a good all-round technical education.

"I left in 1963 at the age of 18 and looked for a training opportunity to do mechanical engineering. I went for interview in London for an advertised job with London Transport. The personnel manager was young, eager and persuasive and steered me towards a career in civil engineering, apparently judging that I was better suited to civil engineering work, focusing on bridges, roads and tunnels, rather than engines, machinery and plant layout. I had never given this sector a thought but I agreed to be indentured to it.

"Many years later I met this personnel manager again when I wrote requesting a replacement for my worn-out sports club tie. He explained and apologised for shifting my career unexpectedly to civil engineering, but the truth of the matter was that, at the time, there were 15 applications for indenture as mechanical engineers and none for civils. He was under instructions to persuade suitable applicants to switch from their first choice to his. I explained that it had all turned out well for me and that I had no regrets.

"During one of my early jobs as a very junior engineer I was placed on site at Tower Hill underground station where we were tasked to move the whole underground station a few hundred metres westward to accommodate a new track layout. This work involved excavating Trinity Square where we soon discovered substantial Roman remains. This slowed down the work and demanded very cautious and painstaking removal of soil, often in the middle of the track. It involved Sir Mortimer Wheeler and a team of other archaeologists. The resident expert on the site tasked me and 'Paddy', who wielded the pick-axe, with careful removal of the soil to expose the foundations of a Roman wall. I was called away to explain something and when I returned I found that Paddy had struck his pick-axe right through nearly 2000 years of history and was continuing to dig beneath it.

Extract from Boudica by Vanessa Collingridge

BOUDICA

what is now Tower Hill station, yet more of the inscription was found lying upside-down as part of the bottom course of the Roman wall. This contained the critical three lines of letters from the base of the inscription that proved beyond doubt that the Classicianus mentioned was indeed the same man that had taken over from the much-hated Catus Decianus, and who in turn had been scorned by Tacitus for disagreeing with the harsh reprisals of Governor Suetonius Paulinus. Although the middle two lines or so are missing, it is possible to read the legend:

DIS
MANIBVS
C.IVL.C.F.FAB.ALPINI.CLASSICIANI
....
....
PROC.PROVINC.BRITANNIAE
IVLIA.INDI.FILIA. PACATA. INDIANA
VXOR F

Inscription on the Roman wall through which Paddy drove his pick.

"Another project was laying the tunnel for the Victoria Line at its junction with other established tunnels at Oxford Circus. The excavation was covered by a steel canopy over which the road traffic flowed.   It was a memorable experience for me, a young engineer, to see the complexity of this engineering of many years standing and the sheer beauty of it.

"I lived in a hostel in World's End, Chelsea, alongside the Thames, when I first went to London.   It was a culture shock after the peace and slower pace of Wymondham in mid Norfolk.   After a year I was sharing a flat with friends in Clapham and I was to live in London for 17 or 18 years in all.

"In 1965, after I had been in London for a few years, I met my future wife, Annie, although we were not to become serious for some time. She came from Edinburgh and was working in the Scottish Office. We eventually got married in 1973 in St Peter's Church, Sheringham, and lived in a second floor flat in Battersea just south of Chelsea Bridge in London.

"Soon after we married I left London Transport and I bought a 30 cwt parcel van and went into the business, buoyant at the time, of delivering hampers to successful competition winners. Annie and I could get 100 hampers into the van and delivered them at 60p each, which earned us a big bonus. Then the three-day week struck and there was no petrol. The business died and I had to do something else. I then worked for a civil engineering agency as a site engineer and offered my services to M. J. Gleeson. I also very quickly realised what a superb training I had received with London Transport, which enabled me to make very good progress contracting. They gave me an initial assignment to assess how good I was and then invited me to join them as a senior engineer, followed very shortly by being promoted to site agent, supervising contracts at the front line. Eventually this led to the last job I completed in London doing a £1.5 million project at the Archway.

"However, we were fed up living in central London. Annie found bringing up two small children very restricting among the traffic and lack of recreation space and we had no wish to move out to suburbia. We found a house in Sheringham and she moved there and I joined her when my assignment with Gleeson's was complete two years later. I was asked to stay on for those two years to earn a substantial bonus, which enabled us to repay some of the bridging loan on the house in Sheringham where we have lived ever since.

"London had its compensations, it was life in the fast lane, and it had been very good to me. I loved to walk around the city – sometimes all day at weekends. There was so much to see and so much history to be found and, when the time came for me to leave, I did shed a tear.

"I returned to Sheringham at Christmas 1979 and for the next six months I had a desperate time trying to get a job. I tried everything including offering to work as a labourer. By May I was ready to pack my bags and return to London. But then I saw an advertisement by North Norfolk district council who wanted a resident civil engineer for its coastal protection responsibilities. After two sets of very nervous interviews I was offered the job, which I gladly accepted. The council retained a consultant engineer, Mr C. English of Mobbs and English, but wanted their own engineer to represent the council. I enjoyed working with Chris English who had been a civil engineer with May and Gurney before he joined Mr Mobbs – a former chief engineer with a water authority - to form Mobbs and English.

" Chris English was a real gent of the old school and often told the story of his army service when he and his unit had to guard the cliffs at Mundesley. They had just one field gun which was situated on the cliff edge and which they polished and kept in mint condition. At the end of the war they were given a single shell to fire – their first – and they invited all the top brass to witness the event. When the gun went off it fell down the cliff. It was straight out of *Dad's Army.*" One dreads to think what invading Germans would have made of that.

"Chris English was magic with water divining rods. He had his own set of brass rods, which could be screwed together and were kept in a mahogany box lined with green baize. On the inside of the lid there was a graph indicating the response of the rods to various depths of water beneath the surface. He managed to produce a water divining map of the Overstrand and Cromer cliffs indicating sources of underground water. Although, as far as I am aware, he always found some water, I was never wholly convinced of the accuracy of the technique.

"In 1988 some of my lifeboatmen, coastguard and fishermen friends put on a show as part of celebrations to mark the 150th anniversary of the Sheringham lifeboat *The Augusta*. These celebrations were organised principally by John Burgess MBE and they included a show by the Augusta Singers, as they called themselves, and who were managed by Val Crowe, a local talented music teacher.

"When the celebrations were over and the Augusta Singers disbanded, a few of them had enjoyed it so much that they decided to start a shanty choir. They had a few songs but no music and Paul Wegg, who was the mechanic of the

Sheringham lifeboat at that time and a good friend of mine, asked me to join them and play guitar for them. (Interestingly, Paul was later to become the mechanic of the Cromer lifeboat. Because of his working hours he was unable to continue in the Sheringham group so he left and formed a new group in Cromer which was to become the 'Cromer Smugglers'.) We struggled for a while to find some songs and a name for ourselves and eventually the name of 'Sheringham Shantymen' was adopted.

" Whilst I have been musical director for a number of years now, one of the many inspirations for our musical repertoire was Bob Roberts – a real life shantyman and master of the Thames Barge the *Canberra*, which was the last working barge to ply up and down the east coast. Bob wrote his own songs, which he played on his squeeze box.

" His wife Sheila owned the cliff-top café in Overstrand and this became a regular meeting place for the local fishing fraternity. The food was excellent, and I would call in when I had the time. Sheila would spoil us all with her home cooking at rock-bottom prices. Sheila, who has now retired, has a book of all Bob's songs, collected over the years, and albums of him and many other shanty singers from all over the world, wherever shanties are sung.

"We decided that our main objective was to enjoy singing shanties and endeavoured to communicate that enthusiasm to audiences large and small who came to hear us, with the RNLI as the main beneficiary of our efforts. There is a subtle line to be drawn between performers enjoying what they are doing for its own sake and entertaining others whilst doing it, and those who do it for financial gain. We have managed to strike that balance and the rigorous selection of Shantymen has much to do with it.

" It is essential that the Shantymen get on with each other and all potential members of the group have to attend for 13 weeks before they are voted to join us, to ensure they fit in. It soon becomes obvious in this trial period whether or not an individual is going to make it, but, none the less, at the end of the 13 weeks each Shantyman has a secret vote. It takes some staying power to make the grade. Applicants must be social animals: it helps if you enjoy a drink, a good laugh and a joke and are serious about being a Shantyman. The Shantymen do not pull their punches and judging new recruits is no exception. The bottom line is we have very few rules – you wanted to become a Shantyman and you are expected to pull your weight without need for reminder.

"Once accepted, new Shantymen need to learn our (current) repertoire of some 120 songs and they soon realise we specialise in harmony of voices and work very hard learning songs by rote. When people pay a fee to hear you, you take on a responsibility to give them value for money. This is different from impromptu singing in a café or pub; yet above all we keep the fun element in what we do, so we don't take ourselves too seriously.

"There are four of us left from the original Shantymen: Ron Newson, Tony Sadler, Billy Thirtle and me, but to be fair to everyone it has always been a growing, changing process and a host of new faces has joined us since those early days and we are the better for it.

"We need 17 or 18 performers for each show to ensure we give people the same quality as they hear on CDs. We always seek to have enough members to call on to be sure that we perform with at least that number. This in itself can restrict our engagements as there are a lot of us and logistically that can be a problem.

" We have moved away from programmes that are exclusively sea shanties and widened our appeal that way. This reflects the range of interests of our members who include a window cleaner, a pilot, a paratrooper, an electrician, a dentist, a doctor, a policeman, a social worker, teachers and some retired and others out of work. None the less, the focus is on enjoyment in all we do and, as a by-product of enjoying our music, we also raise money which we give away to deserving charities but primarily to the RNLI.

"We put on between 40 and 50 performances a year. In the last two and a half years we have raised £20,000 from our performances in village halls, with 50–70 people, to theatres in Hunstanton and King's Lynn with 200–300. The money has purchased a new lifeboat for the RNLI to be called *The Sheringham Shantymen*, which will be based in Wicklow in southern Ireland where it serves the community and where we raised 5000 Euros. Our biggest audience was 1000 in Holland. We have performed in

Norfolk, Virginia, in the USA and are invited back there in 2007. We have had some generous help from a variety of people but especially Henry's of Sheringham who maintain our minibus for us."

Brian is and has been active in Sheringham in many fields. He was an auxiliary coastguard from 1980 to 1995. He is the Hon. Secretary of the Sheringham lifeboat. Now, after 150 years the Hon. Sec. is to become known as 'The Lifeboat Operations Manager', L O M for short! Whatever happened to tradition? He was the first chairman of the twinning association with Otterndorf in Germany. He has been a governor of the primary school and chairman of the governors of the grant-maintained high school. He was a town councillor for six years, the last year as chairman, and is non political. His work as coastal protection engineer at the North Norfolk district council is bringing him into the front line as the east of England tips towards the sea and forecasts of the effect of global warning threaten the sea levels around us.

Brian and Annie have four children. Ben is a teacher and Matt deals in commercial mortgages. Samantha is working in the field of forensic science and Danny is still at university. Brian has a small Pandora yacht moored at Stalham and sailing is a shared family interest.

"I like to co-ordinate and motivate and enjoy my work with The Shantymen where we try to avoid politics. Sometimes we succeed in doing so.

Fakenham and Holt

Nigel Benbow

Nigel Benbow was born in Stiffkey. His father, Brian, has lived there all his life and is one of the hardest working and most helpful of men who would turn his hand to any challenge. He is now 74 and his two sons Nigel and Gerald and his daughter Denise are all involved in the fruit and vegetable business he started from small beginnings. He worked an allotment the other side of the main road from the Stiffkey lamp shop, which at the time was a pub.

Brian had greenhouses there and grew lettuces, vegetables and chrysanthemums. On Friday evenings he and his family would call on every house in the village selling them his fresh produce. They knew everyone from one end of the village to the other. Thirty years ago the council offered Brian a new site on Camping Hill and he moved everything there and carried on the business. As Nigel explains, "He had up to five jobs on the go at one time. He rode a Lambretta, safely for most of the time, except that was, when he met a patch of oil on the road, returning to Stiffkey from Aylsham. He fell off in the skid and broke his ankle. Of more concern was that he squashed the six peaches he was carrying in a bag. One of Brian's five jobs was bait digging and he continued doing so with a broken ankle.

"At one time he had bought an Austin 7 for £125. He did not have a driving licence at the time but drove it none the less. He sold it on later for what he paid for it. He dug graves, was a postman and would respond to any request for help. It was not unusual to have a knock on the door at night to ask if he could dig a grave tomorrow, always by hand and in any of the different soils of the district. I can remember his comments about digging in Wighton cemetery where it was hard chalk soil.

"Gradually he opened shops to sell fruit and vegetables and had six of them at one time. These were at Aylsham, Cromer, where there were two, Sheringham, Holt and Fakenham. This was a heavy commitment for the family and, with my father not getting any younger, we reduced the number of shops to a more manageable three, now at Fakenham, Holt and one at Cromer.

"I was born in Stiffkey in 1957 and went to the village school until they closed it. I then moved on to Wells, which I would reach by bus. I still see some of my old school mates although with the passing years they take some recognising. One might come into the shop and I would feel him staring at me before recalling that we were at school together. I enjoyed school and was an average pupil. However, I have learned a lot more since I left than ever I did as a schoolboy.

"There was not a lot to do growing up in Stiffkey. It was a small village with few amenities and we did not have transport or the money to take us further afield. So we had to make our own pleasures. We spent a lot of time on the marshes swimming and playing hide and seek. We went beach combing which, before the coming of containers, gave good pickings after a storm at sea, when deck cargoes were washed overboard and fetched up along the shoreline. There was some good timber to be had in those days.

" We went fishing for trout and eels in the River Stiffkey. We used wool, impregnated with worms and tied on to our fishing lines to catch eels. They have very sharp teeth, which got caught up in the wool, and could be hauled in. We gathered samphire and winkles and, while I cannot remember finding live ammunition left over from the war, we did find empty artillery shells washed up on the beach.

"We picked strawberries and blackcurrants in the school holidays and there were wild mushrooms around if you knew where to find them. We played a lot in the street outside each other's houses. Camping Hill, where we lived, is steep and I can remember minding my brother in his pram with the dog on a lead, when I let go of the pram instead of the dog and it sped down the hill.

"I have always been good with my hands, particularly with anything electrical. Wayne Scoles and I had teamed up for electrical projects and our teacher gave us an old washing machine. We proceeded to take it apart. The teacher said he did not tell us to do that but as we had done so we had better put it together again. This may have been a try on, but we did it and it worked. If you have working hands you can always be sure of a day's work.

I was at school also with the Curtis brothers – Ian, who now runs horse and cart trips from Holt to Wells, and his brothers Rupert and David. They lived in the house with the honey board outside on the main road through Stiffkey.

"Bait digging was the main occupation at Stiffkey but my father advised me not to make it my career. So I took a job in a shop in Norwich. However, before long I too became a bait digger at Stiffkey. This was in 1975 and I stayed at it for 10 years. It was well organised. Harry Bishop had 13 diggers working for him. He would buy their worms at so much per 100 and then ship them off for sale. The busy months were the cod season from September to December when we might each dig 1500 worms a day. We kept count as we went and never had to count them again when we had finished. I found this ability to keep the score in my head helpful later when running a shop.

"Altogether we dug a huge number of worms in the prime season. Harry Bishop used to load them up in a transit van to take them on for distribution by rail to fishing centres around the coastline. Some days his van was so tightly packed that he had to remove all but the driving seat to fit them in. A transit van full of worms is a lot of worms. We felt we were making a contribution to nature when after our digging the little birds would flock in to pick up the bits and pieces which they would not have found had we not been there. There was a good comradeship among the diggers – the Tidds, Mickey Adcock, Jack and Eric Smith, Michael Snell and Shymu Shepherd among them.

"Another worm digging character was Jack Rowe who kept sheep. Each day he would cut enough grass with a scythe on the marshes to fill a trailer to feed his sheep. There were also some memorable characters in Blakeney. Sid Loose the butcher used to entertain at Rotary and other gatherings. Father grew lettuces for the two brothers who set up Hills stores – Dudley and Kenny Hills. Roger Breeze and John Bone were other characters from Blakeney, which seemed to breed them. Jimmy Temple of Morston was a character with a glass eye. His family ran a pub and ferried visitors to Blakeney Point in his seal boat.

"Although there was a large group of us who dug worms regularly and together on the beach, it was none the less a fairly lonely job. We tended to scatter on the beach to good worm diggings, and anyway we counted as we dug, as we were paid by the hundred, and chatter interrupted the count in your head. We worked on average five hours a day – sometimes because of the tide we took a break in the middle and came back after the ebb later. When we took a tea break in the middle of digging we would gather round sitting on upturned buckets and chat about nothing in particular.

"We liked to go butt forking for fish at low tide. Warham Drift is a gully or low drain on the Stiffkey marshes, with a bank at one end that prevented the fish from escaping. It was a very productive patch to go after flatfish. They swam in at one end and we herded them up to the other where we could spear them. Warham Drift also produced the best quality worms.

"The favourite implement – the butt fork – was made of shark hooks, which Bill Gidney, the blacksmith, straightened out for us and turned into a sort of trident. It was not unusual to catch 200 fish with one of these. We also set beach lines at low tide. We stretched long lines with hooks every 18 inches parallel with the incoming tide. We baited up the hooks and covered them with sand so the seabirds would not get to them before they were covered by the sea. When the tide went out there would be pools along the line where the fish, caught on the hooks, had burrowed down.

"As bait diggers we had to take the rough with the smooth. Demand for bait fell away with the scarcity of fish after Christmas and we could sell only 300–400 worms a day in the next few months. So it was hard to make a living from bait digging all year round.

"Yet people were happy with the village life. It was limited by today's standards but we appreciated what we had. We were happier than many people with much more money and many more possessions are today. The more you have the more you want.

"The village hall was the centre of activity in Stiffkey as there was no pub at the time. There was weekly bingo and events during the year. We played cricket and there was the annual fete, which brought in a lot of visitors.

"After 10 years, in 1985, I had had enough of bait digging and came in to the family fruit and vegetable business full time to run the Fakenham shop. The shop today is much the same as it was then, with the original fitments still in use. My father still buys the flowers and plants and my brother buys the fruit and vegetables. At one time my father would make the trip regularly to Covent Garden and back each day starting out at 3.00 a.m. He still goes to Spalding regularly to buy flowers.

"We specialise in local products where we can. However, this is getting more difficult as small growers close down or contract to supermarkets. At one time we had a choice of six strawberry growers but few are left in the area now. The seasons are ignored by supermarkets. Their consumers have become used to buying any product at any time of year. There are sprouts imported from Australia, carrots from Tasmania and apples from New Zealand. However, we do still have the edge on supermarkets in local products. We buy strawberries, asparagus, sprouts, carrots, beetroot and potatoes whenever they are available locally. These are delivered fresh and direct without going halfway round the world or through a lengthy distribution system. We display seasonal local products outside the shop.

"My girlfriend, Susan Grey, to whom I have been engaged for 20 years, runs the Holt shop. My sister runs the Cromer shop and she has been engaged for 20 years to Susan's brother.

"Altogether we have seven or eight staff. They are all long serving and almost part of the family. The success of our business is the relationship with our customers: 70 per cent of them are regulars. Many of them are elderly and widows and lonely who need a reason to get out of the house and have some human contact in a congenial atmosphere. In the winter they

Susan Gray nearest the shop.

will be in their houses on cold dark evenings from 4 o'clock in the afternoon and they need a reason to be cheered up, even if their main objective is not to buy a load of fruit and vegetables.

"Benbows is where they know they are welcome and can have a chat and a laugh or a moan to a sympathetic ear if they prefer it. This is what independent family businesses do best. We talk and joke with them."

Queuing up to pay at the checkout, over which Nigel presides, is an entertainment and it is not unusual to get involved in the banter:

'How are you, Nigel?'
'Not too bad. Are you alright?'
'Yes, I go to aerobics which does me good at the age of 70. You ought to come with me one evening - it would do you good.'
'You ought to try it when you've been on your feet all day in this shop and see how you feel then…...'

One customer who had been involved in a not too serious argument about prices charged, now shouts out every time he passes the door, 'Dick Turpin'.

And to another regular, making play of scraping together the money to pay for his purchases… *'Fetch the window cleaning fluid – there's a man here who can't pay his bill.'*

Shopping at Benbows is more than a visit to buy fruit and vegetables.

" We are not frightened by the supermarkets because we give our customers something extra. Supermarkets can be a help to us in that customers, who try shopping there, mostly come back to us because they feel pressurised by the pace and don't like the complexity. They miss the atmosphere and service of the small shop where they can buy one orange or a single banana. "

He's right. A recent survey shows that up to 30 per cent of customers who enter a supermarket – particularly the middle aged and elderly - leave it without buying anything because it is too confusing and overwhelming. Price comparisons between small shops, market stalls and supermarkets have shown that supermarkets are the most expensive. None the less, the expansion of supermarkets has had a considerable impact on some parts of the independent trade.

"There are 14 vacant pitches at Swaffham market when a few years ago there was a long waiting list. We have a market stall on a Thursday in Fakenham situated near the HSBC Bank and this is run by my brother. Trade is good. So it is at the shop because we keep our customers loyal and happy despite the opening of a Morrisons on the edge of town. Tesco has also opened a store in town but we will continue to flourish despite it.

"We go to a lot of trouble decorating the shop at Christmas time. After all, it is where I and my staff spend most of our time – considerably more than we spend at home. It is a morale lifter for staff and customers. We have had problems with vandals in the town centre with shop windows being smashed. On one occasion they smashed our main shop window on Christmas Day and I had to be at the shop to secure it from further damage until we could get someone out to board it up. That took up most of Christmas Day. The situation has been better since CCTV was installed in the town centre.

"My main hobby is collecting old tractors and oil engines. I now have over 100 and keep them in a warehouse outside Holt. I also have two 40ft containers for storage. I had a great admiration for Fred Dibnah who died recently. He was a very knowledgeable man whose series on television did a lot for viewers' understanding of the qualities and use of steam and oil engines. He was a former steeplejack and demolition expert of huge industrial chimneys. He was a great admirer of Victorian engineering skills. There were two well known local enthusiasts - Wesley Key who died in 1957 and his son Robert who has died recently.

" I used to have a custom car – a Ford Popular with oversized rear wheels. My brother had a Capri Stardust. They added to our interest in old classic machinery.

" I have never been abroad and never take a holiday. But I do take three days off a year. One is to the Norfolk Show and the other two when I go to the machinery sales at Cambridge. I have three dogs – two alsatians and a retriever.

Henry Sturman

Henry Sturman was born in 1937 at C. T. Bakers ironmongers of Holt where his father, Edward, was foreman to Jimmy Baker. The family lived above the shop. There were three boys at the time and another was born after the war.

"My great grandfather, Henry Arthur Sturman, after whom I was named, died shortly before I was born in 1937 and was head gamekeeper at the Claremont estate near Watton. My grandfather was head gamekeeper for Lord Rothermere at the Study estate near Holt and my father started out as a woods man at Study for a while. He was called up for RAF service on the outbreak of war in 1939 and sent straight to India. He did not return to the UK until the war was over. So I did not get to know him until I was eight years old. He was born a Victorian and his years in the RAF made him a formidable disciplinarian. We moved from Holt when he returned from the war, and he took a job as storeman at Oliver Rix agricultural engineers at Sculthorpe where he worked for Archie Philby and stayed until 1963.

"My father had lost his mother early and grew close to my grandmother.

She had met and married my grandfather when he was gamekeeper at Melton Constable Hall and she was in service there. She was handsome and a fine character.

"Whilst living in Holt, and aged seven, I used to walk a mile to Letheringsett and fish for roach in the Cozens Hardy's lake there. My mother would give me threepence so I could go to a shop in the middle of Holt

Henry's Grandmother Anne Marie

and buy a float, line, hook and two weights all for tuppence three farthings. Then I would attach this tackle to a bamboo cane and bait the hook with rolled bread. I caught a lot of fish and, although we could not eat roach, I was so proud of my catch that I took them home. I was learning fast that you have to think like the quarry you are out to catch. As a keeper in later life this was to stand me in good stead, dealing with everything from stoats to poachers.

"I set snares and traps from an early age - I caught my first jay at the age of six – and all I wanted to be was a keeper. At Sculthorpe school I had little interest in the lessons. My mind wandered off thinking about my traps and longed for the end of the school day. From the age of 11 I would attend shoots as a beater as often as possible, which meant bunking off school perhaps a day or two a week in the season. I would sit up a tree, out of sight, watching my classmates go to school, then climb down and go off to the shoot. My father disapproved when the school complained but my mother always covered for me.

"My grandfather by this time had retired from gamekeeping and lived in Mill Lane, Briston, where he kept 200 chickens and pigs. He taught me how to snare rats. My first attempts saw my snares snapping when they tightened on the rat. I was setting the bender too strong and he showed me how to do it properly. I had a good relationship with him and would usually take him a rabbit.

"Rabbits were an important food, particularly when meat was rationed. We would take one shilling and sixpence to the warriner who lived in a caravan, buy a rabbit and cook it with fat bellied pork. In those days it was reckoned that one keeper could look after 1000 acres. He had to prepare the feed for his dogs and would kill rabbits, gut them and cut off the feet. The rest, including skin and bone, would go into the copper with cabbage leaves, flaked maize and cod liver oil. It was essential to include the skin to counteract the bones. It would set like a pudding but would go off in 48 hours before the days of refrigeration. A keeper also had to make up the pheasant feed, which added to the workload. However, gamekeeping an estate was a big enterprise. My great grandfather, as head keeper, was the right-hand man of the estate owner. He would ride around the estate on a white horse supervising the

36 men working under him. They included warriners who had to supply the rabbits, gamekeepers, mole men and people in charge of silage cutting.

"The rabbits were skinned out and deboned. Then the meat was minced and mixed with meal. Unless it was produced on the estate, maize could be bought from Alley Bros mill in South Creake. They had build up a big business in cornflakes and marketed them under the name of Farmers Glory. Each hen or bantam used for hatching the pheasant eggs knew her own coop and returned to it after roaming in the rearing field which was manned 24 hours a day. Today the pheasant feed is bought ready prepared.

"Whilst the number of birds available to be shot is a measure of the gamekeeper's success there are other factors which he cannot control. The lie of the land and temperature variations are just as important. Birds hate to be cold and will move from high ground to warmer lower ground if the weather is hard. So a gamekeeper with an upland shoot will do less well in certain weather conditions than a colleague lower down.

"At the age of 11 I learned an important lesson. I wanted to buy three bantams, which were on sale at two shillings and sixpence, and I asked my grandfather to lend me the money. He refused, saying that, 'You should earn the money first and then you would have it to spend. You should always live beneath your means. If you do that you will always have money in your pocket. If you spend above your means you never will.' I still apply this today when many people buy on impulse. I see something I would like to buy to replace something I have. Then I think about it and usually come to the conclusion that I don't really need it, so I don't buy it. I only ever bought a new car once. I did this for Edie, my wife, but the dealer went bust soon afterwards.

"I earned money by doing any job on the farm – as a holgee boy, leading horses at harvest and ploughing, mucking out pigs and cattle and food collection. I used to have to saddle the Suffolk Punch who was so large, compared to me, that I would climb on the wall of the manger to get level with him. Otherwise, as I tried to put his collar on he would lift his head up and I could not reach at all.

" The sugar beet required horse hoeing and my job was to lead the horse so the team-man could keep the plough on line to hoe two rows at a time. One time the horse had been slavering down my arm and it was black with flies. I gave my arm a slap to drive them off and this frightened the horse who jumped into the next row. This damaged a number of beet and the team-man had to gather them up and stuff them in his pocket because he would have been fired on the spot if the farmer discovered them. Discipline was that severe at the time. As it was I had to answer to the team-man why the horse had jumped a row. I used to work for David Keith's father, Archie, on the Barsham estate. He would ride a white horse round the estate each morning at 11.00 a.m. sharp. He did not allow smoking and was likely to dismiss any estate worker on the spot for breaking that rule.

"We worked a long day, starting at 7.30 a.m. Then at 8.30 we had 10 minutes for breakfast. We took two bottles with us.

One had tea, milk and sugar, wrapped in a sacking to keep it warm, and another contained cold tea and sugar. We carried a lump of bread and cut off pieces of meat, cheese and onion to eat with it. We carried a clasp knife for this - today we would be arrested for doing so!

"The horses knew their routine. On a Thursday the dealers, who came to buy live poultry from the countryside around, would drive their carts to Fakenham market and then line them up outside a pub. Eventually it was time to return home and many a dealer climbed into the back of his cart and bid the horse to take him home whilst he slept.

"When I left school at 15, I was determined to become a gamekeeper. However, I had to get a job and my first one was on a farm with horses. I soon realised there was more money to be had as a cowman, and left to work with Billy Pointer at his farm in Sculthorpe.

with Tom Gathercole

"Whilst I earned much more money, the job meant that I could not go off with my friends, biking to Wells, because I had to milk the cows.

" When I was 17½ I received my call-up papers for national service. I'd been up since 5.30 that morning and found Billy Pointer waiting for me at the white gate. He had heard that I'd been called for service and told me I could apply for deferment because of my occupation. I told him I'd given this a lot of thought but I'd had enough of his cows and wanted to see what the rest of the world had to offer. This was 1955.

"I loved guns and decided to join the RAF regiment who were responsible for defending airfields and providing ceremonial duties as required. To get this posting I had to join up for four years. After six months' basic training, which included square bashing at Padgate, Lancashire, small arms training at Catterick and an anti aircraft course at RAF Watchet, I was posted to 2nd TAC with BAOR in Germany. This lasted for two and a half years based on Oldenburg and included manoeuvres on Luneburg Heath where hares were plentiful but snaring them was *verboten*. However, camouflaged at night, anything was possible. From this lovely posting we were then sent to RAF Ballykelly, Co. Londonderry, in the Antrim mountains of Northern Ireland.

"This was a quite different environment. For a start you did not know who your enemy was. We would take position on airfield guard duty with a loaded bren gun cocked and ready for action, loaded rifles and a two-inch mortar which fired flares. I got horrible piles sitting on wet sandbags. When I came off duty on one occasion I slept straight through for 24 hours. To relieve the boredom we went in for a little bit of buggerment. We were miles from anywhere and when a hare came to within 50 yards of us I shot it with my rifle. There was just a bit of skin left. The power and velocity of the rifle were such that the bullet left the muzzle at 3500 ft per second, entered the animal and completely blew it apart on exit.

"We also wanted to experiment with the two-inch mortar. This fired a flare to which a parachute was attached and as it came down slowly it lit up the neighbourhood. We wanted to see how far the mortar could reach. So we removed the flare and replaced it with a piece of lead and fired it. There was a tremendous explosion and the shot probably reached Scotland which could just be seen from the Antrim hills.

"For recreation we went into Ballymena where they really know how to entertain visitors in the pub. There was live music with a squeeze box, singing and dancing. Most of the squad were tattooed there and I have some interesting ones on my arms which were applied with two needles and a stick, using blue ink. It was when the tattooist used red ink that the victim suffered from infection. The tattooist was an expert in Andy Capp and I have him on my right arm. I also have a number of less identifiable designs which have lasted through the years."

The reputation of citizens of Ballymena is that they are tight with money but there was little evidence of that. The Revd Ian Paisley tells the story of the vicar who found three halfpennies in the collection plate and asked if there was anyone from Ballymena in the congregation. The answer was, ' No Sir, there are three of us.'

"From RAF Ballykelly we were posted to Felixstowe, close enough to make the trip home frequently. I bought a 650 Triumph Thunderbird motorbike – a powerful machine on which I had to take my driving test. One of the requirements was to keep pace with the instructor walking up a hill without my feet touching the ground.

"After four years' service in the RAF regiment I found it hard to settle into civilian life. I still wanted to be a gamekeeper but initially I joined the Fakenham fire brigade. Then in 1962 the savage winter gave me casual work at the gasworks. I later took a full-time job there as a stoker with eight hours on and 16 hours off. This fitted my availability for the fire brigade.

"I married Edie that year and she helped me to get my first opening as a gamekeeper. She knew the head gamekeeper's wife at the Pynkney Hall estate, home of Mr Anthony Duckworth-Chad, and arranged for me to meet the gamekeeper, Lenny Graver. I asked him if I could do some trapping for him and he said he would check it out. The answer was yes and it was agreed that I should work an agreed amount of acres.

Every day I hung up the vermin I had caught so that Mr D-C could see it when he turned his car. I was approached with a job offer. There would be a cottage, £11 10 shillings a week, a suit of clothes, food for the dog and cartridges. And I could keep all the rabbits I killed (and there were masses of them) and the perks on shoot day. We were very happy.

"The job was going well until I returned with two handfuls of pheasants, picked up at the shoot, when I fell over the fence along the railway line and dislocated my shoulder. The pain was terrible but I carried on as long as I could and then went to have it put back in place. The Indian doctor told me it was going to hurt so I could have an anaesthetic if I wanted it. But I told him to get on with it. He advised me to hold on to him and if the pain got too much, tell him. There were three medics holding me down whilst one of them worked on putting my shoulder back in place and the pain was unimaginable. At one point I tightened my grip on the doctor and lifted him off the floor and across the bed, kicking the others, who knows where, in the process. So they finished the job with an anaesthetic.

"For a month after that I had my arm strapped to my chest. I had my snares out and one day I spotted a man among them. I went out after him and saw him run off towards Peddars Way. Then he disappeared. There was no sign of anyone but I listened and heard the brambles rustle. He had holed up in the middle of a bramble bush. I saw the outline of a gun under his coat and I ran after him, tripping him up and eventually subduing him. I pulled off his water boots and told him he could get them back if he swapped them for some identification. The gun by this time had disappeared.

"We got to the Hall where Mr D-C was living on his own. There was no one else around and we sent for PC Bob Shooter from Fakenham. He arrived in 10 minutes and searched our captive in the kitchen. He found no evidence and concluded that I had arrested an innocent man. So we would have to let him go for want of evidence. However, I insisted I had seen his gun before I caught him and he had obviously hidden it. So we had better go and find it. By this time, head keeper Lenny Graver had joined us and it was a chaotic scene.

"It was getting dark by now but we all trooped out and I identified the bramble patches in which the gun was most likely to have been hidden. Eventually we found it and unloaded the cartridge. When confronted by this the poacher admitted his guilt. He went to court and was fined £36, which was a heavy fine in those days.

"I stayed at the Pynkney estate until 1965 and then moved to the Trowse estate of Timothy Colman. We lived at Crown Point at Arminghall. The estate was close to Norwich and the lights of the city made it nearly as bright as day during the night. One evening Edie saw five men walking the sugar beet and shooting. I went out and found their car parked by a gravel pit. I took note of its make, colour and number and went to meet the five poachers as they approached it. On my demand they emptied their pockets and the birds were laid on the ground. Then they challenged me to come and pick them up, raising their gun butts as they did so. It was time to back off. I contacted PC Black at Poringland who said he would make a visit to the city where he apprehended four of them. They went to court, pleaded guilty and cried their eyes out.

"Edie was lonely at Arminghall and we moved on to the Wills estate at Ousden between Bury St Edmunds and Newmarket. We had a brand new house, centrally heated, and I was the only gamekeeper for 2000 acres. While this was double the acreage traditionally serviced by a gamekeeper, I had the advantage of a vehicle, although there were many parts of it that could only be approached on foot. The money was good and we reared enough birds for eight shoots each with eight guns.

Henry with his son Keith at Ousden

"Wills estates then started to asset strip and cut down many of the trees. They left the perimeter trees of a wood but cut out the middle and still expected to provide shooting for the same number of paying syndicates. I did not think much of this and was declared redundant. So after nine years I left and took the head keeper's job at Hilborough. We had a lovely house there and, over the next two or three years, met some very distinguished people who came to shoot. These included royalty and a number of Americans among whom were Frank Borman, pioneer of moon landings, and Henry Ford IV.

"The owner of the Hilborough estate, Madam, as she liked to be called, entertained her guests at length for lunch on shooting days. On one occasion they did not emerge until nearly 3.30 p.m. when the light was fading and there were two drives to go. Needless to say they were not a great success. Madam said, 'That was a bit disappointing, Sturman.' There was no point in arguing about it as she was always right.

"In 1980 I heard of a job going at Blue Stone farm at Sculthorpe. I worked there for 18 years with John Sexton, initially over 1100 acres which was increased to 2000 acres later. When the farm was sold I decided to move no more as a gamekeeper. Edie was ill. She has suffered from Parkinsons for 24 years. To make things worse, she had a fall and cracked her pelvis, requiring a six-hour operation to repair the socket which held her hip bone. The delay in having this operation caused her a lot of pain and now, after 10 years, it needs replacing. She is not strong enough to undergo it and it has left her disabled and in great pain. Constant painkillers do little to help and produce their own side-effects.

"After Bluestone was sold I went into business on my own account, exterminating vermin for many clients at farms, grain stores, gardens, shops and restaurants. I catch rats, moles and vermin of all sorts, using my long experience of thinking like the quarry.

"Setting up one's own business is full of challenges. I had to work hard to master the new regulations dealing with poisons, so that I could gain certificates of competence required by law. In the first few years I never had a contract with my clients, but recently I have been asked to sign one, following a tightening up of disease control. All contractors on farm units must be monitored under new EU regulations. I look after rodent control at poultry rearing farms, potato stores and cattle yards. The control of disease means that there must be no cross infection from one unit to another. Spraying boots and clothing is essential to ensure disease is not cross transmitted.

"When I have, or rather make, the time from boring administration, I lay aside my pen and tie fishing flies. But being a countryman, time has never meant anything. I have been at work at 3.30 in the morning, sorting out a pair of crows who were making a great noise attacking their own reflection in the windows of a barn conversion. I shot one and the other was shielded by a tree so I said I would come back and finish the job. The owner asked if I could come later in the morning next time but of course the crows were gone by then."

Henry and Edie have four children – two boys and two girls - and 14 grandchildren. Their younger son, Mark, has followed his father into the vermin control business where he has not far to look to learn the tricks of the trade. None the less, they avoid treading on each other's toes.

"With all my moves, if it wasn't for Pynkney Hall, which was a very happy time, I would not be where I am today. I had the best of gamekeeping in the days when an estate owner invited his friends and each went away with a brace of birds. For all of us on the estate a shooting day was like a family occasion and the guns would not dream of paying for the shooting – although if they had a good day they might be inclined to reward the gamekeeper and his team. Estate owners reciprocated with invitations to return hospitality. Today it is a commercial enterprise. A brace of birds costs £25 to the guns, many of whom have little understanding of the countryside."

Henry is well liked and respected. He is a perfectionist and never rests until the job is complete. Always neat and tidy and well turned out, he takes a pride in the career in which he feels fulfilled.

North Creake
and
Burnham Market

Sylvia and George Thompson

Sylvia and George Thompson have, between them, lived in North Norfolk for over 150 years. They have been married to each other for 57 of those years. Sylvia was born at West Acre High House. Her father came from Harpley and when she was eight years old the family moved to the Shammer estate. Her father became the 'team-man' – responsible for the horses - for Mr Tony Everitt. Sylvia, born in 1924, was the only child, and she went to school in North Creake from the age of eight until she was 14 years old. One of her jobs before she went to school each morning was to fetch the milk for the household from the dairy. She was a star pupil in English and poetry and gave recitations in a concert each year – an experience which would stand her in good stead for life.

"We children from Shammer and Cuckoo Lodge had to take packed lunches to school and at playtime I would go across the road to Mrs Howell where she would fill a kettle with water from a pump in the yard. Mr Poppleton, our headmaster, would boil it on an open fire so that we could have a hot cup of cocoa with our lunch.

"I remember one night in summer, my mother woke me and got me out of bed and took me outside to see the northern lights – a sight I have never forgotten. When I was 12 years old I went to Stocksbridge near Sheffield for the five weeks summer holiday. While I was there I was taken round a working steel mill – what an experience for a country lass. I was too young to be allowed to go down a coal mine with my cousin when we visited Bakewell. I had to write about my visit when we got back to school. I also remember when at Harpley school, at the age of six or seven, seeing the R101 airship go by. The number on it was so plain I can still see it in my mind's eye.

"I looked forward to treats during school years such as cycling to Burnham with my parents some Saturday evenings to the Cosy Cinema. Little did I know that my future husband was also there. Also we made Sunday trips to London once or twice a year by train from Burnham.

"I had wanted to be a teacher but did not pass the eleven-plus so I applied for the job of cook to Dr Jolley of The Hollies in Snettisham. With the outbreak of war the duties of running the house fell more and more to me. Even though I had no brothers and sisters I was certainly not spoiled as a child. The normal condition in my family was hard work. During the war Mrs Jolley, a trained nurse, was required at the Lynn hospital. They had two very young children and I was given the task of looking after them and running the house including the cooking. This was a heavy responsibility at the age of 14 and I had to grow up fast.

"We had an occasional reminder that there was an active war on. For example when a dog fight took place in the skies above, and bullets punched holes in the tin roof of the British Legion hut. The most frightening memory was the doodle bug which droned overhead and suddenly went quiet, crashing down to explode nearby. We had a red party-line emergency phone as this was the doctor's house. If there was an emergency I had to report it to the ARP. There was a US army camp on the Snettisham beach and the Canadians were at Hunstanton. Inglisthorpe Manor had been turned into a hospital and several other large houses had been commandeered.

"The Hollies had a big kitchen and the WI used it for canning fruit and vegetables grown nearby. They managed to find cans which we filled, lidded and sealed and then sterilised in boiling water in the copper. Dr Jolley distanced himself from this, but it turned out to be safe enough and he was never called upon to use his medical skills for any mishap. Canning food in this way would not be allowed today but then nor would much else that went on in wartime. We were probably healthier then than many people are now. We did not eat between meals but we ate sponge and suet puddings. They were good for us then but, according to the experts, they are bad for us now. It is surprising we ever survived at all.

"We were all encouraged by the WI and other organisations to raise money to support our troops. I borrowed a barrel organ from the hospital and, with a friend, played it in the streets during War Weapons Week. We didn't have an organ grinder's monkey but we collected money for the war effort.

On my days off I cycled home to North Creake which is 16 miles from Snettisham. My father used to cycle with me on the return journey to Snettisham to make sure that I made the journey safely in the dark and in the icy weather. You were not allowed to show a light on a bicycle more than a slit, because of the blackout. My father had to cycle back to North Creake and was up again at 4.30 a.m. next day. He died aged 68 and had been fading for a while." As George recalls, "The night he died I had hit my head on the stairway. He said, 'You gave your head a real rattle' and then he died."

"My father was a remarkable man with a love of poetry and he kindled my love of it from an early age. Every night he would say a poem with me from a picture showing a mother cat pushing a pram containing twin kittens and a little boy cat walking beside it. I can remember to this day:

Boy cat says:
Which way are we going Ma - when shall we be back?
May I have a little ride after Jill and Jack?
Is this road the proper road, have you lost your way?
Do you think it's going to rain any time this day?

Grandpa says he knows a boy who bothers all his friends
With a list of questions Ma, that he never ends.
Sent his grandma off her head, made his grandpa lame
Oh! It would be horrible if I did the same.

"I came home from Snettisham after seven years in the job, but I was ill for a year. When I had recovered I took a job as a nursery nurse at Stow Langtoft Hall, Suffolk. This was a

London County Council home for orphaned and abandoned children. I was not there long because I could not work with the matron and moved on to Creake Abbey as cook to Admiral and Mrs Thursfield.

"In 1947 I went to a dance and met George for the first time. He was home on leave from the army where he served in the Royal Engineers in Greece and Palestine for three years from the end of the war. I took time to make up my mind about getting married to George. He was a joker and it took a bit of getting used to, but my mother really liked him – he was the son she never had - and we just grew together. We saw each other every day.

"We were married in North Creake church in 1949 followed by a reception for over 100 at the village hall. "In 2009 we will

with 1949 page and bridesmaid – David Mountain and Sheila Roper

celebrate our diamond wedding. We took rooms at Cross House until we found a home in Burnham Road where we lived for seven years and then moved to a house in the Paddock and later to Dunns Lane where we have lived ever since."

George was born in Burnham Market in 1927. He went to Burnham Market School where his family lived in the lane alongside. His father, Jack, born in Weasenham, was a blacksmith and set up at Satchells.

"My first job was with the butcher Charlie Wright where I delivered orders on a bike or by horse and cart. I moved on to be an operator at the Cosy Cinema and then took a job with J. F. Williamson of Fakenham as a builder's labourer. This was too far to cycle every day and I moved to work for Brian Rowland. We built the Airey houses in North Creake, which were only expected to last for 10 years. They have been there now for 57 years.

"There were three fish and chip shops in Burnham Market in those days. We would creep up the Goosebec, which flowed in a drain under Harry Farrow's shop, and pretend to be ghosts, terrifying his customers with our catawaulin'. We used to cheek Skip Guinea, asking him if he ever cut his fingernails by mistake whilst he was trimming his fish portions ever smaller. He used lard to fry his fish and thick-cut slices of potato giving them a flavour that you just don't get today. We used to gather round the table in his shop and Grandma Guinea, who was disabled, would suddenly make an appearance. Although she was good hearted, if she caught us perched on the table she would say, 'Tables were made for glasses – not bloody arses.'

"Dick Raisbury used to travel round the village with the 'night cart', better known as the 'honey cart'. He was used to objections about the smell but he told one customer, who irritated him more than most, that the smell came from the contents of her bucket and he would put it back so she could empty it herself. I met him at the style one time in Station Road when he had a full bucket in either hand. He said he wanted to buy a pint of milk and I put it in his pocket so as to keep my hands clean.

"From working with Brian Rowland, I took a job as a milkman and for many years delivered to half of Burnham Market, getting up at 4.15 a.m. and cycling to Burnham Market to start my round at 4.45 a.m. My first call was Alfie Bishop in Creake Road and then I worked down the Overy Road, up Friars Lane and down Herrings Lane. I also served Sussex Farm, which was best when the weather was fine, and the Moorings Hotel at Overy Staithe. George Phillips was a big buyer of milk and cream and was fed up opening 80 bottles of milk a day and little cartons of cream. So I agreed with him and the dairy to supply both in churns. His wife was delightful and the Moorings was a famous hotel.

"Every day I would pass the time of day with Jimmy Riches, owner of the village store. He told me once that he was driving with his son, who was visiting at the time from Hong Kong on a trip to Cromer, when there was impatient hooting from behind and a car overtook him at angry speed. When they arrived at Cromer they saw the car parked in front of them and Jimmy Riches asked him why he was in such a great hurry. The driver replied that he wanted to see the sea.

Jimmy said it had been there for all of his 80 years and he had never had a problem finding it.

"I delivered milk each day to Captain Woodget, the retired Master of the *Cutty Sark* who lived at Flagstaff House, Burnham Overy Staithe. One morning he said to me, 'You didn't call on me yesterday – I was looking out for you.' I said I had been on a trip to London and visited his old ship in dry dock at Greenwich. 'What did you think of her?' he asked. I said I was surprised how cramped it was below decks and how little headroom there was. Captain Woodget replied, 'That's why we are all round shouldered.'

"There were bombs aimed at Norton church and the oil depot, during the war. There were two masts erected nearby and at night they had winking lights on them and the enemy took an interest in them."

George and Sylvia's daughter Nicola was born in 1953 on Easter Sunday. Dr Luffman said she must be sure to avoid Easter Monday because he was going away. As it happened Sylvia phoned the doctor on Easter Sunday to say the birth was imminent and, because she needed an anaesthetist his partner, Dr Woodsend, was also summoned and took the call in his bath. He assured her he would be with her in North Creake from Burnham Market in 15 minutes, and he was.

"Dr Sharp was another character at the Burnham surgery. He was know as 'one-arm Jack' because he had a water pump in his back yard and the joke was he topped up his prescriptions with this free ingredient. Whatever the truth of it he was a very good doctor and he provided very good cures."

Sylvia settled down to village life – very different from conditions today. "I would go out with the pram and it could take all afternoon. First I met one friend, then another. We all knew each other. No one locked their houses and there were six or seven shops in the village. You could buy bread and groceries, there was a post office and drapery store and a cobbler's shop. Now there are no shops and we have to go into Fakenham every week and sometimes to King's Lynn. I joined the Mothers Union, the WI and the Young Wives and served on all three committees. Mrs Elliott, the vicar's wife, started a drama group and we would put on a show once or twice a year.

"For 40 years I did the flowers in the church and made jams and cakes and bottled fruit for the fetes. The church was an important centre of village life, with its own vicar. Now it is part of a group ministry of six or seven churches and North Creake has a very small congregation. George went to evensong in the late 1950s. There was a choir of 12 and he was the only one in the pews. North Creake was traditionally high church and South Creake low church. One way for the visitor to tell high or low is the number of steps up to the altar. High church has five steps. Low church would more likely have three.

"Where village families used to live there are now second homes, empty most of the time, and many of the owners do not get involved in the village when they are here.

"However, in 1998 we started an annual Christmas show and this has helped to bring the village together again, with residents and second-homers taking part to put on shows of a high standard. I played in all of these until I reached the age of 80, which is the upper age limit insurance companies are prepared to cover.

Back row: Betty Sculley, Sheila Upjohn, Ben Honniball, Geoffrey Kemp
Second Row: Richard & Jill Ellis, Win Collinson, Doris Gandy, Pam Green,
Barbara Allen, Jane Faires, Philip Quinn, - Winkie, John Green
Front Row: Rosemary Pooley, Marjorie Johnson, Sylvia, Yvonne Autie, Myrtle Grey

"The first of the shows was *The Fair Maid of Creake*, which was performed by WI members and written by Sheila Upjohn and Ben Honniball. In the following years we put on *Cinderella*, then *Dick Whittington*."

Ben Honniball pays his own tribute to Sylvia and George:

"When I first moved into the village, I was told to be very wary of Sylvia as she could be a little fierce! Consequently when meeting her for the first time I was very cautious – how wrong could I be. She was most welcoming and helpful and she and George have been my very good friends ever since.

"When I formed the Creakes drama group, Sylvia appeared in the first production and since that time has appeared in all the Christmas productions and an Olde Time Music Hall. Our audiences love her, especially appreciate her Norfolk dialect and give her a good ovation. I remember, with joy, her role as bargewoman in *The Wind in the Willows* and her other little cameo parts over the years. Sadly, age comes to us all, and terms and conditions of our insurance prohibit Sylvia from appearing on stage, but she and George still remain stalwart members of the group, enjoy watching us in rehearsal and assisting us in other ways. At the monthly music and poetry group Sylvia has a fondness for Pam Ayres and regularly reads pieces of her poetry in the Norfolk dialect:

"I'll dream about me apple cheeked old mather,
Her smiling face above a pot of broth,
She used to cook us every sort of pudden
Proper puddens in a pudden cloth.
When we come home from school all cold and hungry,
One look along the clothes line was enough,
And if the pudden cloth was there a-flappin,
We all knew what it meant – a suet duff.

A suet duff would set your cheeks a-glowing,
Suet duff and custard in a mound,
And even if you'd run about all morning,
A suet duff would stick you to the ground.

She used to make us lovely apple puddens,
She'd boil them all the morning on the stove.
If you bit on something hard that wasn't apple,
The chances were you'd bitten on a clove.

Or else there'd be a grit jam roly poly,
We'd watch it going underneath the knife,
And if you took a bite a bit too early
The red hot jam would scar your mouth for life.

Sylvia recalls, "My favourite show was *Toad of Toad Hall* – 'Cor!
Thas a luvly day in't' - and we did *Snow White*, *Aladdin* and *Jack
and the Beanstalk*. Apart from the new kitchen and toilets the
village hall is much as I remember it more than 70 years ago.
It was where the girls of the village learned to dance."

Nicola is married and lives in Sprowston near Norwich. She
was a dispenser at Boots for 27 years until they had a number

with Nicola and husband John

of redundancies. However, it was not long before they asked her to come back and she is happily back in her job. Her husband John is a chef on the oil rigs and made the magnificent cake for Sylvia and George's golden wedding in 1999.

King's Lynn

Alan Gajdzik

Alan Gajdzik's family - father, mother and four sisters - moved to Norfolk 35 years ago from the Reigate area of Surrey. Alan went to school there and left at the age of 15. He worked for a local jeweller for nine months and then joined the family in King's Lynn. His father, a skilled and qualified baker, had bought Ridouts bakery in Sir Lewis Street. Alan was the second oldest of the five children and the family lived at the bakery. Later the bakery shop was moved to Loke Road, close by, and now has the name *Yummies* above the door.

"My father was born in Poland in 1925 and apprenticed to a baker from the age of 12. He and his brothers, who were brought up on a small farm, were an industrious family. One became a butcher who started in a tiny shop, yet today that business employs 400 people. The German occupation of Poland during the war was a very turbulent time. In 1947 at the age of 18 my father emigrated to Reigate in Surrey, where there was a small Polish community. He spoke no English and went to work for my Uncle Joe who owned a bakery in Brixton.

"My mother's father came from Wales. He was a lifelong serious socialist and regular reader of the communist daily newspaper. None the less, I got on very well with him and he was an influence in my life. Among other things he was a keen racing enthusiast, took me to Epsom races and taught me how to gamble on the horses. He also believed in hard work with a social conscience and reinforced that family ethic in me. I have inherited it from both sides of the family, which is well balanced, generally fulfilled and has done exceptionally well.

"My teacher at school, despairing of my academic performance, said it was a waste of time my staying on and I might as well go and get a job. In fact I enjoyed school but learned very little there. I have learned much more since. When the end of my schooling was approaching I went for a series of job interviews and, with the help of my aunt Gill, got the job advertised for a young male sales assistant at a local jeweller with whom I worked for nine months. I was not allowed to handle any merchandise worth more than £10, but I learned the trade. I then decided to join my family in Norfolk and made the three and a half hour journey by train to King's Lynn on a cold, wet Sunday in March. I fell asleep in the train and the guard woke me up when we were in a siding at King's Lynn station.

"As I left the station I expected to meet people who could direct me to Sir Lewis Street but the town seemed strangely deserted. For the first time I saw a row of terraced houses. I had left my friends behind and it was a wrench for all the family. My sister, Lynn, the eldest, had already moved to live in France, whilst Krysia, Helen and Colette were at school in King's Lynn. It was soon evident that if you go to school in the town and enter its sporting activities it does not take long to get to know everyone. The town is like a magnet and I was to discover later from my frontline view at the Country Line Buffet at the railway station that if you come from King's Lynn you always return.

"I went to work at Ridouts bakery, by this time owned by my father. It was very hard work. The ovens were coal fired and we started at 3.00 a.m. Dough was mixed by machine, then cut and moulded by hand, in the traditional way, to make loaves and rolls. My mother worked a full day in the Gaywood shop and helped my dad in the evenings making cakes. We had a trade bike – Granville style – and my job was to deliver bakery goods to the homes of some of our 400 customers. The business had two shops at the time – Ridouts cake shop in Gaywood and the baker's shop at the main bakery in Sir Lewis Street.

"I stayed for eight months and then decided to leave home and return to Reigate. My parents, always open and fair minded, were prepared to go along with this so I went to stay with my Uncle Dave. However, when I burned a hole in his settee with a cigarette, I was asked to leave and moved in with Grandad. I then went to work for a jeweller in Croydon where I was subsequently offered, but turned down, the job of assistant manager. I feared this would lock me in to the business and it would be difficult to break free. So I left the shop and went to Hatton Garden – the centre of the diamond trade – where I walked into City Jewellers who gave me a job.

This was an entirely different experience. The quality and price of the merchandise was in another league. For example, the shop had a £1.5 million window display and one of the most beautiful pieces of jewellery I ever saw was a six-carat heart-shaped diamond valued at £96,000. I was earning £25 per week.

"I stayed for 18 months and then tired of the jewellery trade. I was restless to fulfil my hankering to be self employed. This was in 1975 when I was 19 years old, and I have been self employed ever since. This, of course, makes one unemployable so it is sink or swim. Whilst working at Hatton Garden I met Betsy at a party and the relationship developed. She was working in an estate agency.

" I did a number of odd jobs on leaving Hatton Garden and took my friend Jimmy, who was suffering from depression, to Devon for a break. We were both at the same primary school from the age of five and are still good friends today. Among other things during our stay in Devon, we ran a kiosk on the beach in Paignton. When I returned I took a job at the Mother's Pride bakery in Crawley. My uncle Trevor, who was a van driver, worked there too. At an early age he introduced me to football at Crystal Palace – a team I have supported ever since through good times and bad. My own prowess at football was confined to playing at school. I attempted to play after I left school but the deterrent was the size of the goalkeeper so I decided to be a spectator from then on."

When Crystal Palace made it to the Cup Final against Manchester United, Alan's loyalty to the club was tested.

" I queued for 18 hours for two tickets to Wembley from 10.00 p.m. one evening, all through the night, to 3.00 p.m. the next day, by which time the tickets available were either at £10 or £75.   I chose the £75 and then found myself in Wembley stadium, by chance sitting next to a friend I had not seen for years.   I have been to seven out of Crystal Palace's top 10 matches over the years.

"In 1975 I received a phone call from my mother asking if I was interested in taking the concession for the café on the boating lake in Hunstanton.   At the age of 19 this was to be my first serious experience of self employment and a new challenge.   The café was rented from the council for a period of four years and I ran it with Betsy's help between April and October each year, working in the bakery when the café closed down for the winter.   Betsy had moved up to Norfolk in 1976.

" We had some good fun running this business for holiday makers.   I painted a name on the back of each chair such as Elvis, Miss Piggy etc. and customers would make for the chair that suited them.   It was chaotic at times as they would move the chairs around with positive intentions to enhance their images or with more negative intentions, for example, when a large lady might find herself sitting on the Miss Piggy chair.   It was the sort of thing one could get away with at the seaside among happy holiday makers.

"Betsy and I faced a period of very hard work.   The day started at 8.00 a.m. loading the van at the bakery with cakes and rolls and delivering them to the boating lake café where we served the customers all day. Cakes and snacks were big business for us - we would sell 22,000 cakes over the summer, plus doughnuts and egg custard tarts, all made at Ridouts bakery in King's Lynn. The bakery was busy supplying wholesale and door-to-door house sales and our own two shops.

" It has always been difficult to get trained bakery staff in the King's Lynn area, particularly those who could make quality products from scratch. Fortunately we had my brother-in-law Delly and another skilled worker in Jonathan Rose working with us. Jonathan now has his own bakery in the Wisbech area. Unlike most bakers today, we still make our own puff pastry, starting with fat and flour, rather than buy it in ready to use. We supplied Woolworths in King's Lynn and their Hunstanton branch, where we had a concession instore, until Woolworth discontinued food sales in all their branches. We then opened a shop in Norfolk Street, King's Lynn, in which my mum and Betsy worked until 2005 when it closed.

"The boating lake café had its problems from time to time such as the serious flood in 1977 when we were inundated with six feet of water. None the less, it was a successful business and there were opportunities to extend our menu. I decided to serve simple cooked dishes, freshly made, well presented and plenty of it on the plate.

"I went to Cambridge on a course, one day a week for three years, to study for my City and Guilds qualification in baking. By this time my sister Krysia was playing an active part in the bakery which she now runs. She also runs the Gaywood cake shop. Betsy loves working there on Saturday mornings, which she has done for 20 years, serving and chatting to the loyal customers who made it a destination not to be missed. My sister Helen owns and runs Yummies in the Loke Road.

" We tendered for and won the concession to supply the film crews for the epic *Revolution*. King's Lynn was the film set depicting 18th century Philadelphia. For six months we supplied 1500 rolls a day, all of which had to be cut and buttered by Betsy and Mum between midnight and 3.00 a.m., and a similar quantity of individual cakes. They had to be delivered early in the morning and the contract was at a set price.

"A great parade was part of the film and the build up to it swelled the demand to 3000 rolls and 3000 cakes a day. The parade took place along King Street and the costumes were magnificent. As it turned out the film was not a great box office success but it was a great experience for us. There were other sequences filmed at West Tofts in Thetford Forest and my first attempt to find the 'derelict village' built for the film set found me in the midst of unconnected large-scale army manoeuvres with much shooting involved.

"In the winter of 1979/80 I was asked back to participate in the jewellery trade show in London. I wish I had been on commission. I was their top salesman, working for £45 per week. The sale of just one £400 ring would enable my employers to pay my salary for a week.

"When our concession at the boating lake café expired in 1979 I concentrated on the bakery for the first half of the 1980s. In 1986 my family saw an advertisement for a tender to take on the Country Line buffet at King's Lynn railway station. The question arose, if we were to go for it, whether it

should be part of the bakery business or whether I should undertake it as a venture of my own. I was advised by my Uncle Trevor that if I was going to do it I should be the proprietor, otherwise I would be saddled with all the work for a wage.

" It was a big risk for me, but I put in a bid and Betsy said that if I did not want it I was sure to get it! The bid was successful and I signed a three-year lease with a five-year bank loan. That combination is not to be recommended. Our house was already mortgaged and for years I had to continue to work at the bakery to subsidise the buffet.

"We had some major problems to contend with about which we could do very little. For example, when the line was being electrified to save the train service from King's Lynn station, buses took over from the trains for two years. We also had nine months of scaffolding on the building and a rail strike, all of which affected the business. It did not get better until 1990 and meantime I still had to work at the bakery to subsidise the buffet. I would start work at the bakery at 3.30 a.m. and then on to the buffet for 8.30 a.m., finishing at 3.00 p.m.

"It was 1998 before I could take my first holiday when Betsy and our two children, Alex and Hayley, and my brother-in-law Steve with his family, took off for three weeks to Disneyland in Florida. Up to that time I had not been an admirer, from a distance, of aspects of American life. I had never been to America. However, I was impressed with the efficiency and punctuality to be found at Disneyland and the interest taken in serving their customers. This added to customer happiness and satisfaction with the service. Taking an interest in and engaging with one's customers is a feature of businesses I run and my staff are keen to do the same. It is most effective if it is genuine and comes naturally.

"We had planned our holiday months ahead. This enabled me to order up supplies to cover my absence, brief the staff and arrange cover. The kids had priced up the sweets. The preparations to be away for two to three weeks were exhausting but they produced a peace of mind and I could switch off during my holiday. I returned fired up with ideas. I changed up the tables and chairs and put new equipment in the kitchen so we could develop the bacon and filled rolls trade. It was a busy time with the construction of the Morrisons supermarket nearby and we had builders to feed as well as train passengers. I used my cooking skills once more to build a reputation for good value, freshly cooked food. I continued to do some work at the bakery and agreed that taking over Dad's old Mercedes, which he did not use much, would be payment in kind for my labours.

"It helps to tell the customers what you are doing for them. For example, that you have put a napkin in the bag with the food, where they can locate accompaniments for it, and ensure that the food on the plate looks attractive, is hot, good value and plentiful. It is not difficult to be polite. I genuinely enjoy my job and want the staff to do so too. This has a considerable positive effect on the customers. One meets all sorts in a station buffet but I hate any sort of discrimination and all are welcome – and made to feel welcome. The clientele changes on a Friday and through the weekend.

"Most of our regular customers come from outside King's Lynn and many from Dereham, Holt, Fakenham and other towns, who have a choice either to catch the train from Norwich or from King's Lynn. They choose the latter because the service to London is faster, parking has improved and they like coming into the buffet. We have built a loyal clientele who like our coffee, our rolls and pastries, made freshly in the family bakery, and at prices which in many cases have been stable for three years.

"We serve them with minimum delay so that they can be sure to catch their trains. With most train journeys from King's Lynn lasting a minimum of one hour they have a good choice of reading material, neatly displayed. I don't like my customers to have cause for complaint. I like serving happy people. This requires some nurturing and the individual approach to them leads to a good relationship. Both Alex and Hayley have worked with me in the buffet and I believe it has helped them to understand and relate to people.

"In 2002 Betsy and I got married. We had lived together for 26 years by that time. We have a son, Alex, who is 21, who, following a course in business studies, is now seeking a career with a blue chip company. Our daughter Hayley is 19 and working in a resort in Spain in the Pirate Show for children which puts on six performances a week. Neither of us was particularly motivated

to enter into marriage and the children rather revelled in the fact that they were not of the stereotype of many of their contemporaries' families.

"None the less, the environment of Las Vegas provided examples of the best and the worst wedding chapels and we decided, having found an ideal venue, to get married there and then. So we invested in a $50 licence and sought out the Reverend who was positive that, having been living together for 26 years by that time, we would be certain of our choice.

"The girls had just invested in new dresses and it seemed a pity if we did not take advantage of that. So I bought a shirt and a ring. We returned from the ceremony by bus, had no reception and resumed our holiday. Such response as there was from friends was mainly of surprise because they thought we had been married for many years. My family could not believe it at first but then my sisters arranged a surprise party to celebrate the news. Betsy's mum, brother and niece came up for the celebrations.

"Each year at Christmas Betsy and I, with Alex and Hayley, Betsy's brothers Steve and Robert and their children and Uncle Ray go to London to spend an evening at the Golden Nugget Casino in Shaftesbury Avenue. We started a tradition that when each of this family gathering reaches the age of 18 he or she gets £100 to spend at will. Steve has three boys and Robert has a daughter. Then the adults gamble and share the pot four ways if there are any winnings. One year, after the pot had already been paid out, I had an inspiration of my own and won £150. There was some mild dispute as to whether this was part of the pot and thus should be shared out. However, to make progress, Uncle Ray said he had been given a tip for a horse. I suggested that we would put £40 of my winnings on it and, if it won, share the proceeds four ways. Everyone was happy – particularly as the horse came in at 20 to 1 and we were £800 to the good.

"At my brother-in-law's suggestion we bought a greyhound with the winnings. We named it Casino Wizard, for obvious reasons, and kennelled him at Hove where he turned out to be a really good dog. He only runs at Hove, where he has raced 100 times, winning on 18 occasions and coming second in another 30. We each have a trophy. We have also invested in a pup called Casino Valentine because she was born on St Valentine's day. She is now 18 months old and ready to begin a racing career of her own and of which we have high hopes. It costs about £50 per month to keep a dog in training and we are getting good sport and good value for money.

"My four sisters are all busy. Lynn, the eldest, lives in Paris and works for a heart monitoring company. Krysia and her husband Delly run the Ridout Bakery and the Gaywood cake shop. Helen owns the Yummies shop in Loke Road and Colette is busy bringing up her young family.

"Father died in 2000 and we returned his ashes to Poland. This has strengthened our ties with the family who still live there. Mother is still going strong. We are a close family where hard work is a family characteristic. It also helps to have a rational view of problems. I will worry about something for one day and then let it go. This way one can be contented and happy with what you are doing. I would be happy to continue to run the buffet for the rest of my working days.